A Survivor's Story

Prisoner of War
to
Parish Priest

John Hanson Read (1917–2004)

A Survivor's Story

Prisoner of War
to
Parish Priest

By

John H. Read

With a preface by

Frances Read

Edgerton Publishing Services

Pett, East Sussex

First published in Great Britain in 2007 by
Edgerton Publishing Services
Jasmine Cottage, Elm Lane, Pett, Hastings, East Sussex TN35 4JD
Tel. +44 (0) 1424 813003
Email enquiries@eps-edge.demon.co.uk

Reprinted digitally with minor corrections in 2008

ISBN-13: 978-0-9548390-3-1
ISBN-10: 0-978390-3-X

A CIP catalogue record for this book is available from the British Library.

Typeset in Sabon by Edgerton Publishing Services.

Printed and bound in Great Britain by
JEM Digital Print Services, Sittingbourne, Great Britain

Contents

List of illustrations

Preface

John started work on these memoirs in December 2001. He had had two weeks in the Conquest Hospital in Hastings after a severe angina attack, and when he got home he badly needed a project. So I suggested that he sorted out his Prisoner of War memoirs.

As I anticipated, his answer was that in the first place no-one would be interested, and that anyway he had long ago chucked out his notebook. To both of these objections I had an answer. First, it would mean a great deal to the family and close friends, and second that I had rescued the notebook, which I produced, much to his amazement.

This notebook, closely written in pencil on both sides of the pages (see Figs 9 and 10 on pages 18 and 19), was standard U.S. Forces issue – the Service Writing Tablet, acquired in Manila, along with U.S. navy cutlery. (The fork is still in constant use in our kitchen.) John wrote up his experiences, from capture at the fall of Singapore to release from the Funatsu Camp, on the second stage of his journey home, on the U.S. Navy ship *Marine Shark*. This was within three weeks of release. The sketches included in the book were also done on this voyage. Observant readers will notice that the sketches have a corner missing. In the difficult early months after repatriation John threw his book of sketches onto a bonfire in his parents' garden at Tunbridge Wells. Fortunately he thought better of it and rescued them before too much damage was done.

To many readers this will be the most interesting part of this short book, and some may well skip the "before and after" chapters. They do, of course, fill in the picture for those who knew John after the war. I had to use considerable persuasion to get him to agree to these further chapters.

Like many other Prisoners of War, and especially those who suffered in the Far East, John didn't talk about his experiences for many years. It wasn't until the early 1980s, nearing retirement, when he was Rector of Guestling and Pett, that we realised he could talk about those three and a half years. Our daughter Judy, walking the dog, was amazed to meet a neighbour who said what an interesting talk he had had with John about his time on the Burma Railway. When he agreed to preach for the local Burma Star Association, we knew the ghosts were well and truly laid.

John was not one to dwell on the horrors of his captivity. The reader will read between the lines. What is undeniable, and typical of his whole approach to life, is that he made the best of things. The Prisoner of War Medal (Fig.25 on page 74), issued to prisoners of war in all sectors, incorporates barbed wire as a symbol of captivity. The medal is worn below the campaign medals and it carries on the reverse the wording "Intrepid against all adversity", which would perhaps have made a good alternative title to John's memoirs.

When John asked me to marry him, I knew that I loved him, but I did have two concerns. Would I be able to support him properly in his ministry? Would I be able to help him through any possible after-effects of his years in captivity? My parents had given us four girls a fine example of service to the community and to the church, and the three clergy wives I knew were all happy people. That seemed an encouragement. As for the war years, I had been evacuated with my youngest sister Mary, and was then away at boarding school. Our eldest sister, Joan, served in the Wrens, based on Portland Bill. Our sister Mardi nursed war-wounded at St Thomas's. We had all been at home in Eastbourne during air-raids at night and the more frightening hit-and-run raids in broad daylight. I was really only aware of the war in Europe. I knew nothing of the Burma Railway and the possibility of recurrent nightmares and malaria. But John was such a positive and outgoing person, that I quickly decided to follow my heart and soon realised that God had it all planned.

John was a great encourager, and interested in everyone and everything. His last weekend in July 2004 was typical. On the

Saturday we were at Five Villages House (our local sheltered housing) to celebrate their 25th anniversary, and he talked to everyone. On the Sunday afternoon we took an elderly friend to visit the Giant Steam Engines at the Brede Valley Waterworks on their Centenary, where they both had a great time.

John died on 19th July 2004, aged eighty seven. He had a major heart-attack in the early hours, and died in the Conquest Hospital. John had not quite completed writing up the latter years of his retirement, although we had discussed headings, so I have done this for him, as best I could. It has been an emotional experience, and has helped me through the early months of bereavement. Truly a labour of love.

The Service of Remembrance and Thanksgiving for John's life was led by Bishop Peter Ball in Icklesham church. There was standing room only. John is buried in Icklesham churchyard, which he loved. He had often said Matins walking among the headstones if he found the church locked. A few months later we were invited back to St Mary's, Beddington, for a memorial service there, a moving occasion after 26 years.

As a family, we all think that John was special. We know that he was a faithful and much-loved Parish Priest. He and I had 52 happy years of marriage. As a father, he listened to our children, often took their advice, and gave them confidence that they could tackle most things. His ability to make amazing things out of bits and pieces was a winner with our grandchildren. And they all knew that he prayed for them every day. He was also a favourite and supportive uncle and great uncle, and the wider family meant a lot to him. We are all thankful that everyone can remember him in good form. We all thank God for him.

Thanks and appreciation are due to many people for their encouragement, advice and practical help. In the first place to my sister, Mary Dawes, who typed the PoW years for John and encouraged him that this was a worth-while project. Thanks also to Jane Horne, a local friend, who typed up the Early Years section. I am grateful to Imogen Clout, a dear friend, for allowing her tribute to be appended. And I am indebted to Stuart Malin, married to John's god-daughter Lindsey, who really got me going after John's death, and (thanks to his expertise) enabled me to complete these memoirs. Finally, my thanks to David Penfold (Edgerton Publishing Services) for agreeing to publish the book and particularly for the cover design.

Frances Read
Icklesham
January 2007

1

Early Life

Bath

I appear as a new born baby with my twin brother, George, on 8th June 1917. Here we are, in the arms of our father, Arthur Read. We are in the garden of No. 4 Evelyn Terrace, Bath. My father is in uniform, back from Belgium. He was in the Artists Rifles, a City regiment. Family tradition has it that this undemonstrative man ran down the road shouting "It's twins". No scans in those days.

Fig. 1. The twins in their father's arms.

George and I were baptised in the local mission church, Emmanuel, Weston, Bath on 13th July 1917. This was a "tin" church (corrugated iron). It was bombed along with much of Bath, and destroyed in 1940. The cracked font now grows daffodils in the churchyard.

Father was on the staff of the National Provincial Bank. He was moved about quite a lot and came, via Tiverton, Norwood and Hunstanton, to Stamford. Later on to West Bournemouth.

Bournemouth

The family now numbered five children: Elizabeth, then George and me, Christopher and lastly Susan. I was always proud of our large family. But quite a bit of time we were looked after by housekeepers as our mother was ill with tuberculosis. For her convalescence, Mother lived in a cosy wooden bungalow on Heath Common, Storrington. We had happy visits there.

Fig. 2. Mother Read with the twins.

Fig. 3. The five Read children (from left): John, Susan, Elizabeth, Christopher and George.

Fig. 4. The twins: George and John (with puppy).

3

In Bournemouth we lived in a pleasant house in Chester Road, Branksome, not too far from the sea at Branksome Chine. There were happy times down at our beach hut.

Elizabeth went to Bournemouth High School. She was to spend many happy years there and made lifelong friends. George and I went to Hayley Prep School. In the short time that I was there, I managed to get into trouble. The bully of a son of the head-master (Lamb) provoked me. I took one of the white ink wells which fitted into a hole in the desks and threw it, ink and all, at him. My first (not by any means my last) beating followed.

Westminster

However, I was not there long as I was taken off to Westminster Abbey for a voice trial. This must have been very largely my aunt Dorothy's doing. She was a well known piano and music teacher for long years at Downe House Girls School near Newbury.

The Song School at Westminster Abbey is in the cloisters. There, aged nine and bewildered, I met Sydney Nicholson, organist and choir master. He later founded the Royal School of Church Music (RSCM). My test piece was the song *In Scarlet Town where I was born*. I was accepted and in due time appeared as a proba-tioner in "A" choir (boarders) and as a pupil in the Abbey Choir School in Deans Yard. There I remained from 1926 to 1932 progressing through "Singing Boy" to "Chorister" and to "Head Chorister".

Westminster is a long way from Bournemouth. In my early days I was certainly pretty homesick. I spent quite a lot of time in the sick room. It probably did not help very much that holidays at home were much shorter than ordinary schools. This was because of Abbey duties with choral matins and evensong every day and the demands of rehearsals. With four other children in the family, I sus-pect that this presented some problems not only for me, feeling hard done by, but also for the family. I could throw some long-lasting glooms. It didn't help that this would be put down to "liver".

Fig. 5. Chorister at Westminster Abbey.

Holidays

Father and Aunt Dorothy took us on some famous holidays. There was the splendid yacht on the Norfolk Broads. Also some fairly hair-raising expeditions in the old green caravan. Burton Bradstock was a favourite place. We even found ourselves in Harlech once.

George

Back at the Abbey I did, of course, miss my twin brother George. One unrecognised affliction for me was that I not only missed him, but also in my imagination I would generate scenes in which George was being ill treated. How could a ten year old explain the lump in my throat, and could therefore not sing? For this I was beaten. Not by Mr Nicholson or Mr Peasgood, the sub organist. No, that was by Dr Bullock, the next organist. I did deserve the beating I got for letting off a cap pistol in the pocket of my red cassock in choir practice! Dr Bullock was not one for explanations. Those piecing black eyes of his haunt me to this day.

Scouting

I was a very keen scout, badges and all. And from scouting I am sure that I learnt the art of making do, smiling and whistling etc. The scout camps at Bletchley near the village of Bow Brick Hill were absolute bliss. We had visits there from Sydney Nicholson and Osborne Peasgood, the much loved sub-organist. One of Nicholson's hymns *We sing the praise of him who died* has as its tune "Bow Brick Hill". So Nicholson liked the place, too. I can remember watching him chopping firewood. Our camp consisted of three converted railway carriages. I have had a fond feeling for such ever since. There are still plenty to be seen along the south coast near Pagham Harbour and Winchelsea Beach.

Back in choir we were kept pretty busy. There were all the services and essential choir practices as well as ordinary school work.

Some of my misdemeanours were punished, others were not found out. There was, in those days, a covered roof space at the top of the five-storey red-brick choir school building. "Roof" looked out over Dean's Yard and over to Victoria Tower. The soot and grime of London collected up there, but it was a very welcome playground on wet days. Cricket and football were either on Dean's Yard Green or on the Westminster School sports ground in Vincent Square.

Choir School and Cloister

Quite how it came about I do not know, but I got the reputation of being able to mend things. Sadly, I was at one time forbidden to "mend" any more five shilling pocket watches, which we used to buy from Samuels, the jewellers. I did, however, manage to fix up my own radio. For the aerial I had bedsprings, and for the earth the hot water pipes in the dormitory. It was on this radio that I learnt to love Jack Payne and his Orchestra with the theme tune *Say it with music*. I also heard, one night, news of the German invasion of Czechoslovakia, and even at that age experienced alarm.

Six years of concentrated liturgy, prayer, psalmody, Bible and sermon must have sunk in. Twelve years later, as a prisoner of war, I would recall such verses as *I had rather be a doorkeeper in the house of my God than to dwell in the tents of ungodliness*. The door in question in my mind's eye was the south cloister door into the nave of the Abbey through which we processed from Song School.

One of the privileges of being a chorister was that we would see and meet interesting people. I was not around for a coronation, but I sang at the wedding of the Duke of Kent and the beautiful Princess Marina. There was also a big Service of Thanksgiving for the recovery from illness of King George V.

I was confirmed by Bishop Hordern of Lewes in Henry VII Chapel (Lady Chapel).

There had always been a connection between the Abbey and Abyssinia. One of the processional crosses which I admired was Abyssinian, made of pierced brass. So it came about that at a scout parade in Dean's Yard, we were "inspected" by Emperor Haile Selassie. I still have a strong feeling for Ethiopia and support things there with prayer and giving for hospital work, especially amongst women. Years later, I found such a cross in St Mark's Church in Horsham, where I served my second curacy.

Hurstpierpoint

I was still singing treble at the age of fifteen. But then, as did quite a lot of ex-choristers, I went to St John's College, a Woodard Foundation, in the country outside the village of Hurst. My best friend, Gerald Gray, had already gone there, so I felt quite at home.

School days can, of course, throw up characters among staff as well as boys. The interesting ones for me were those who made music. One long lasting friend was Basil Roper-Cook. He was adept at plying the saw with a fiddle bow. Rude enough boys called him "septic sawrer". For some reason I was called Borstal.

Hawkey

But it was Horace Hawkins (Hawkey) who taught French, German and geography and, above all, music, who stands out. He had a Sorbonne degree in organ playing and had studied with Widor. It was in his room off the draughty cloisters that we music people found refuge.

There would be a fire going in the grate, brass instruments hanging on stout pegs all round the walls and that three-legged armchair propped up on the fire surround. This all added up to a great sense of privilege for us few. I took to the cornet. Bugle also in the O.T.C. band.

Having that French background, Hawkey would have the whole school bellowing French music for the communion services by such as Henri Potiron, choir master at Sacré Coeur (ribaldry). On one famous occasion, Hawkey leaned out from the organ seat and addressed the assembled cornets, horns and trombones in a loud voice: "Brass, blast you. More noise!" One way of getting fortissimo! It was all good fun. I gravitated to the trumpet given to me by my Aunt Mildred, and played in the orchestra for Shakespeare plays.

Hawkey went on to become organist and choirmaster at Chichester Cathedral. He was there to play at my ordination to the priesthood years later. This after the passage of twelve years and a whole wartime experience.

Mention of the Shakespeare plays brings in my brother Christopher. He too had come to Hurst from choir school at Salisbury Cathedral. He was a pretty bright chap. He got cast in female roles in the plays. Had, he reminds us, once to learn some Welsh as Lady Mortimer.

I was lucky enough not to get caught in various escapades round the countryside with my gang. We never harmed anyone, though I don't think the farmers would have been very pleased had they known.

O.T.C. and Exams

The Officers' Training Corps (O.T.C.) figured quite large of course. As a bugler I would take part in early morning reveille and last post on training days. Last post sounding out across the front quad and out into the countryside was appreciated by residents quite far off. To the extent that when one dim headmaster later cancelled it, there were regrets.

I preferred shooting up on Welcome Bottom Range near Danny Hill. We felt quite manly setting off on the school rifle-range bus with our .303 (SMLE) rifles across our knees. I thereby got out of playing too much cricket.

The results of the School Certificate exams were posted on the board in the cloisters. I feared the worst, when someone said "You'd better go and look at the board". I seem to recall a lot of red ink; but anyway it said credits in the subjects: Latin, French, English, Spanish and arithmetic, and beside these the words "exemption from matric". This exemption qualified me for Oxford years later.

Paris

I would put in here that Hawkey used to take us singers (double quartet) to sing in cathedrals and famous churches in Paris: Notre Dame, St Sulpice, etc. It was quite a lively time politically and one evening cars were set on fire outside our hotel in Boulevard St Germaine. But we were also taken to an elegant *appartement* and there introduced to Monsieur Widor, no less. Old and bald with very thick glasses. Beside him stood Monsieur Marcel Dupré, organist of Notre Dame Cathedral.

At Hurst

We used to have quite a length of free time on Sundays. It was then, after lunch, that we would make a point of getting into the country-side and to go as far as was possible in the time in each direction. This once took us up to the Downs to a certain quarry. Amongst other things to be "found" there was, I remember, a very old derelict lorry. Somehow we managed to extract large ball bearings from the wheel hubs. No-one else seemed to want them – so! Another time we made it to Burgess Hill. Most memorable of all was the finding of an old paraffin stove in a dilapidated barn down by the flood stream known as Fludders. We acquired some bread and some butter and there were quite delicious fry-ups. We heard later that the farmer knew all about this and rather envied us.

In the centre of the flood stream was a rather alarming brick hole built up to water level and acting as an overflow for the mill stream. One of the tests for the gang was somehow to get out on the edge of this and walk round it. The drop was only a few feet though it seemed more.

Another time we made it to Cowfold, where there is a monas-tery for Trappist monks. No harm done there. But on the way there was an old shed which needed investigating. When a fearful old woman came out screaming, we departed.

On a less disreputable level, we boys did achieve quite aston-ishing things in the Shakespeare productions. I was not on the stage, being in the orchestra pit. Brother Christopher made his great hit as Lady Mortimer. I still have a photo of him. But the really memorable performance was given by my very good friend, Basil Roper-Cooke, as the king in Henry IV Part 1. I can almost hear him still. "So shaken as we are, so wan with care." Basil was a fine figure of a boy, looked the part and understood it well. He and I were in the second row of the scrum in the first fifteen. With our scrum caps on we looked fierce.

The City

There came a day when the careers master got a letter from a bank in the City. The Mercantile Bank of India. Had he got two boys who, after School Certificate exams, could be interviewed for a job. Please send photos! So I, and a boy called Wink, duly found Grace-church Street – with the help of a policeman. I got the job.

I remember ringing up home, a thing unheard of in those days, and telling father. He, as a banker, was delighted. I don't recall having any time between leaving school and "the City".

The Roper-Cookes

Here is a very sincere note of gratitude to Fred and Emily Roper-Cooke, Basil's parents, for saying I could go and live with them in Acol Road, West End Lane, West Hampstead. It was a great blessing for me for the next four years. I was soon part of a cheerful group, enjoying badminton, dancing and, if we were lucky enough to have the loan of a parental car, expeditions into the country.

Some of the happiest times I can remember were being with Basil, home on leave from the R.A.F., when we would take our-selves off to Hampstead Heath with the dog. He once brought home the contents of an air-force sea marker. This included a lot of aluminium powder. It would not only burn but spread like anything over the waves. So we must try to burn some. Next morning all the nearby chickens were aluminium plated.

Looking back, I hope I managed to show some gratitude to the Roper-Cookes for giving me so secure and loving a base. Church at St Mary's on Sundays. There was always plenty of music, with Mrs R.C. at the piano with hymns and songs of an evening.

The Mercantile Bank of India

At the bank, my first impression was the smell of the place. Whether disinfectant or polish I never did find out. But of course, the old fashioned counters were of lovely mahogany, the cashier's grill very solid brass. My first jobs were in the downstairs correspondence department. It was chiefly a matter of filing letters and so getting to know the names of firms. Many addresses seemed to be in Scotland in such places as Arbroath and Dundee, where presumably the many Scottish directors and share-holders lived. There were always a lot of Scotsmen both in head office and in the Far East. The names of Yule and Catto were prominent. It was they who had started business, chiefly in the jute trade in Calcutta. My job included putting outward letters through the franking machine, filing and generally getting to know things.

I had been encouraged by Father to see my job, though humble, as part of the great work of the city. He would tell me to take a walk after lunch at a Mecca Café. To stroll on to London Bridge and take a look over the parapet at the Pool of London, Hayes Wharf, and all the cranes and shipping, tugs and lighters. A splendid sight.

One really got the idea of what a so-called Merchant Bank was for in the Outward Bills department. A marvellous variety of things shipped from this country to India, Ceylon, Malaya and China. But every shipment had to have its documents: invoice, insurance, bill of lading, bill of exchange. These would, in due course, be sent out by Imperial Airways flying boat. I once nearly got the sack by sending the Calcutta documents to Bombay. One had to initial each item as one put it in to the blue air packet. All honour to the general manager before whom I had to appear. He said "Just don't do it again" and commented that I had not tried to fib my way out of it . . . For there was my initial. I didn't tell him that I was in love with a Swedish girl.

As one worked one's way up the head office, one eventually came to be on "the general ledger". That was a fearsome job, for every transaction (double entry book keeping) in a dozen or more departments had to be entered each day and balanced! That inevitably meant late hours, but also overtime pay. The City is a very special place after hours. There's a nice pub in Leadenhall Market just across the road from the bank! Then it would be home to West Hampstead *via* Moorgate and Baker Street. Then either 53 bus from outside the head office of Abbey National, or train to West Hampstead.

I was kept fairly busy with studying for the Banker's Institute exams, but there was relaxation too, mainly in music-making. With the London Junior Orchestra at the Royal Academy there were weekly rehearsals. I was second or third trumpet. Dear old Ernest Read (no relation) ran this full orchestra and conducted concerts there. I had a few paid engagements. One of these was a mass performance of Handel's *Messiah* in the old Crystal Palace. Once, while studying in my room in Hampstead, I saw the sky all red. The Crystal Palace was burning down! Another time, I was asked by one Gerald Ellison, a professional, to play in the orchestra for Gilbert and Sullivan's *Patience*.

For a short time, I was in the chorus of the Richmond Operatic Society. I was also a member of the Purcell Club at the Abbey. This was for old Choristers. We gave recitals which included madrigals. We were also asked to sing grace at the annual dinner of the Goldsmiths Livery Company. Very generous they were too.

Posting to the Far East

At the age of 21 I was called into the office of Mr Burns, the Accountant, and informed I was posted to Penang in the Straits Settlements (Malaya). That was more or less expected. So it was off to Austin Reed's to buy tropical kit. This included the proverbial Palm Beach suit. Not much worn, in fact, for local Chinese made white ducks, which were the usual rig in Malaya.

All this was done without much consideration for my family, nor particularly for my brother, George. In fact, the excitement of it all and of the voyage out in SS Canton on her maiden voyage, left me, I am sorry to say, very full of myself.

Burnt into my memory to this day, is the recollection of George waving goodbye to me from the steps of his bank in Hove. I was in our car and recall looking back to see him. The family in general were quite used to seeing their members off either to India or to schools.

George's Death

It was after I had been transferred to Kuala Lumpur that I got the awful telegram. It was April of 1938. George had been killed when

Fig. 6. George, as a pilot in RAFVR.

his Hawker Hart trainer crashed into the South Downs. He was a Sergeant Pilot in the R.A.F. Volunteer Reserve. There is little doubt that he would have been in the Battle of Britain within a year or two.

I went through every emotion: shock, guilt, darkness of mind, protest against God. The very clouds seemed so damned unconcerned. I would look up to the sky and wonder where George was now.

St Mary's Church, Kuala Lumpur, was just over the road from the Selangor Club where I was living in bachelor quarters. So it was there, in the company of the excellent chaplain, that I spent a long time and had much comfort and wisdom. Life had to go on. I still have a fine poem that my friend, Basil, wrote for Mother and Father. It spoke of the bugles that echoed towards the Downs by the village of Streat where George, and now Mother, are buried.

Basil himself was killed in January 1941 when his plane crashed into a mountain on an island off the west coast of Scotland.

Mother was not alone in her grief. Before long she had the war and its consequences to cope with. She would not be one to take it all serenely. And next was Christopher's near-death accident in the submarine H.M.S. *Upholder* in Malta. Then followed the fall of Singapore and me a prisoner of the Japs.

Elizabeth was in her first teaching post at the convent school in Ditchingham, Norfolk. She also had responsibility for the convent pigs. Bird watching once, she was arrested for spying.

Susan was doing splendid work in the Land Army in various places, especially in Inkpen, Berks. In Kent, she was in a working party which was machine gunned by a German plane. They had to dive into a ditch.

War in the East

I was back in Penang when war was declared in Europe. It was quite a long while after that the Japs blasted Pearl Harbour and their tyranny spread all over the Pacific.

Like most members of the European staffs of the banks and firms in Penang, I had joined the Straits Settlements Volunteer Force (5th Battalion). We were trained in the use of Vickers 303 machine guns. Our job was to assist the police in case of riots. In the event we had to man beach posts. I held the rank of sergeant. We had local Malays as other ranks. They mostly disappeared when things got serious.

Fig. 7. John as a Sergeant in the Straits Settlement
Volunteer Force.

Then came the day when we volunteers were rung up as we sat in our offices and told to report immediately to Volunteer HQ in Penang.

We were sent to war, as it were, by the charming Mrs Aste, wife of the manager of the Penang branch of the Mercantile Bank.

2

Prisoner of War

Recollections written just after release by John Hanson Read, Sergeant, Straits Settlement Volunteer Force, on board US Troopship Marine Shark *in mid-Pacific, October 1945*

Fig. 8. On board USTS *Marine Shark* in Pacific Ocean, 15/10/45. I spent most of my time encamped up this companion-way behind the bridge. Crew let me alone – just stepped over me. Appreciated solitude.

Fig. 9. The notebook.

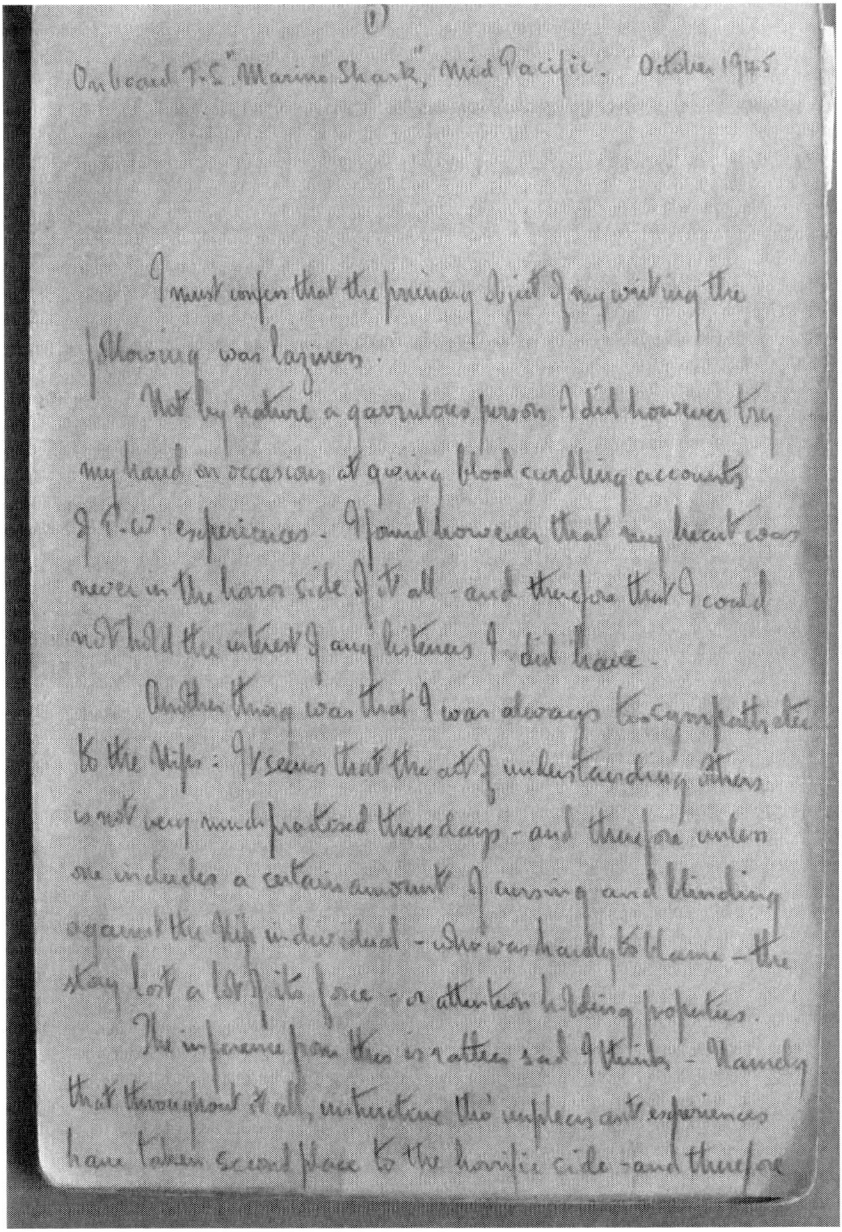

(1)

On board T.S "Marine Shark", Mid Pacific.   October 1945

I must confess that the primary object of my writing the following was laziness.

Not by nature a garrulous person I did however try my hand on occasions at giving blood curdling accounts of P.-W. experiences. I found however that my heart was never in the horror side of it all — and therefore that I could not hold the interest of any listeners I did have.

Another thing was that I was always too sympathetic to the ships: It seems that the act of understanding others is not very much practised these days — and therefore unless one includes a certain amount of cursing and blinding against the Jap individual — who was hardly to blame — the story lost a lot of its force — or attention holding properties.

The inference from this is rather sad I think — Namely that throughout it all, instinctive this unpleasant experiences have taken second place to the horrific side — and therefore

Fig. 10. The first page of the notebook.

19

First Days of Freedom

I must confess that one object of my writing this was to get some delicious solitude. But also to get some of the story down in writing for my family. Not by nature a garrulous person, I did however try my hand on occasions at giving blood-curdling accounts of PoW experiences, but I found that my heart was never in the horror side of it all and that I could not hold the interest of any listeners I did have.

Another thing was that I was always too sympathetic to the Nips in their broad situation. It seems that the act of understanding others is not very much practised, and therefore, unless one includes a certain amount of cursing and blinding against the Nip individual – who was hardly to blame – the story lost a lot of its force or attention-holding properties. The inference of this is rather sad, I think: namely, that throughout it all instructive though unpleasant experiences have taken second place to the horrific side, and nothing but hate is left after three and a half years. So perhaps my rather unsociable withdrawal to privacy may provide a view of the non-horrific side of PoW life under the Japs.

I know perfectly well that it is an interesting story. I pray that I may be helped to write it in an interesting manner. Any attempt to relate it by word of mouth would be hopeless – it's too long. I trust that through a runaway tongue I do not misrepresent the story.

This effort is primarily for loved-ones at home. I hope they will forgive me for even daring to suggest that their interest in the doings of one they love could be as short-lived as that of others. It will be one of the joys in store for me to have the attention of these loved ones and I hope I shall not be found to have taxed their patience.

I hope that any reader may be able to detect throughout the story the part my up-bringing has played in making the life more bearable both for myself and perhaps for some others. For this I have to thank my dear parents. Even as far back as scouting days I remember trying to see the reason for irksome duties, while others grumbled. In the O.T.C. at Hurstpierpoint College I seemed to be one of the few who tried to do things properly, and enjoyed it. I found an extra interest in training as a bugler – you will see how that very bugling was of use later. As a volunteer in the Straits Settlement Volunteer Force I always made a point of entering right into the spirit of training schemes – this was in the extended training period. Others rushed off home at every opportunity, while I hardly went out of camp except as a soldier on a pass.

All this sounds very righteous. I can't help it, it's true. I thank God I recognised the truth of matters and had the gumption to obey that knowledge so early on. It is part of my make up, for which I claim no credit. Also, at some unrecognised period of my upbringing or education, I had acquired the invaluable ability of abstracting myself from any present circumstances. But the faculty of being able to see myself at any moment, particularly unpleasant ones, through other eyes, or as seen on a stage as an event that has happened and finished, was, I think, my saving grace. I am not widely read, and have just the ordinary public school Matric sort of knowledge. Apart from music and choral experience I only thought of myself as fairly ordinary. So I can only think I have just inherited this power of abstracting myself.

Lastly – and it should have been firstly – one thing only made life bearable, namely hope. In proportion as one had hope, one lived or died. And heaven knows there were enough things to die of. It wasn't until near the end of my captivity that I came to the conclusion that it was nothing else than an inborn trust in the Lord's providence that enabled me, sometimes anyway, almost to enjoy myself.

I never even thought of myself as a good person. I didn't like excesses, though probably indulged sometimes. Regular church-going kept me more or less on the straight and narrow, though here again my faith was none too strong. It was music that drew me, being always in choirs. Something like force of habit made me unwilling to let a good habit drop off. This landed me in trouble, as you will read, in Funatsu, Japan.

It was not until the Funatsu days, when we truly were in straightened circumstances, that I realised fully that my trust had all along been subconsciously in God. In Funatsu that realisation came to me so strongly and intimately and personally that the visible outward signs eventually caused me to be considered un-hinged.

You will read and judge. I will try to write it as completely as possible.

Penang

It was the first of December 1941. I was sitting in the Penang branch office of the Mercantile Bank of India totting up balance figures. The phone rang and I was told to report to Volunteer HQ immediately with all my kit. I left the long columns of figures with a bit of a smirk. What did they matter now? As it happens, they were useless and lost within a fortnight.

Within a few days Jap planes were over us as we camped in the Sports Club grounds. We thought about slit trenches then, and while digging them, watched Butterworth, on the mainland, being bombed. Through my telescope I watched one plane dive in flames, which I later discovered was one of the only two we had there. The camp got too hot when they machine-gunned our huts and tents, so we were moved out to beach posts. I was in charge of one such post just beyond my house in Tanjong Balik along the coast from Georgetown.

I had eight Malays and five Europeans, two Vickers 303 machine guns, and a land line connection with HQ. There was a certain air of unreality about it all, but at least we were getting down to things and it was quite a challenge to make the best of the situation. Beach posts were made of the trunks of coconut palm trees – double rows of trunks a foot thick stuck into the sand, roofed, with a doorway to the rear and slits for firing through. Training had got one into the way of coping with discomfort.

One dark evening rations were brought in from a dump on the roadside by one of the Malays. In the dixies were pork for the Europeans and beef for Malays. Aforesaid Malay nearly died of remorse when he found he had actually carried pig. And of course they would not touch their beef. That evening we Tuans had a royal feast.

Fig. 11. JHR (Sgt.) and two other volunteers – outside Sergeants' Mess
Cookhouse. Penang 1940.

On the horizon in early dawn on 17th December there appeared some odd-looking boats with tattered sails. Ah, I thought,
training our two Vickers over that way, Japs masquerading! Not a
bit of it – they were East Surreys, Gurkhas and Leicesters crammed
into native boats. Thank heaven we held our fire. They landed right
by us. Japanese blood on the Gurkhas' kukris. Wiped them on the
grass.

We were giving them coffee when the field telephone went.
"All stores out on road. Immediate withdrawal." Resigned remarks
from the regulars – "We've heard that one before somewhere." We
retired, I past my own home, a Chinese house shared with three
other chaps, down to the town. Food and kit, more than we could
use, dished out under big trees in some Tuan Besar's house. A long
convoy was eventually collected and to the accompaniment of a
violent thunderstorm we went down to the docks. Pitch blackness,
lightning flashes our only illumination. But what a scene those
flashes showed. A lot of equipment which was never loaded onto

the commandeered ferry for lack of willing hands. I was one of CSM Watts' party of volunteers and helped load the last object – a motorcycle.

Penang wrecked, flaming and stinking. It was more blitzed than any other town in Malaya. The storm was our saving, as the Nips still bombarded the town after we had left. They didn't realise we had gone, apparently, for they didn't enter the town until two days later.

The ferry was very much overcrowded. I slept a little – my bed a kitbag on which I half sat, leaning at an angle on the stern plates within a couple of feet of the propeller shaft – until I was called to clean anti-aircraft small arms against daylight. We were not attacked and so the top deck did not collapse, as it might have done, under the effect of several automatics firing. In two days, with thunderstorms all the way, we were in Singapore. The military element were sent to 7 M.R.C. I had a bunk to myself, which struck me as very comfortable – my first reward for having three stripes. Civilians were badly received. I got virtually bombed out of Singapore town, though not before an excellent Christmas service in the Cathedral. I sang in the choir one Sunday.

My services were then required at India Lines, Changi. This was to train Asiatic volunteers and was very strenuous as I had to learn most of what I was teaching. When the Japs took Pulau Berani, an island across the water, we moved, because they had mortars. I was assigned a pill-box on the main road on a bridge on the perimeter of Kalang aerodrome. A large bomb-crater showed what the Nips thought of it. Malays would retire gracefully under the gun platform to pray when bombs fell, then run away. Then we were withdrawn from the pill-box and put in a ditch with just rifles. I collected a long anti-tank rifle, which fortunately I did not have to fire – the recoil is pretty hefty.

The ditch formed the fifteenth line of defence of Singapore, so we were told. I put a bit of floor in my ditch and dug it out a bit. While waiting I found a copy of *Esquire* and lay there under a lovely blue sky shaded by a tree. Shells screaming back and forth. Was that really me, in such an extraordinary situation? Not for long, however, for dear old Captain Fisher of our 3rd Battalion from Penang came up, fell us all in on the road, and tearfully told us of the capitulation. The taps had already run dry – the Nips had got the reservoir. The date was 15th February 1942.

Capture

After acquiring a few clothes and edibles from hastily deserted houses in the area, I had a lovely night's sleep in a soft bed. All lights were on. Wonder of wonders, no Nips appeared. Heaven knows what they would have done. Just didn't think. It was while relaxing in that nice house that I met another English chap. Our discussion about the situation went like this: in wars people either got killed or wounded or were taken prisoner; who were we to imagine otherwise; now the thing was – how to go on as a prisoner. Little did we know. We were rounded up by our own people. Threw rifles and suchlike in a heap on the lawn of the Chinese residence where we spent the next night.

I met my first Nip when I was sent with some message along to another group. Thank heavens I had been warned to stop, bow, and then proceed firmly.

The next morning we started the fifteen-mile march to Changi. A pretty miserable hike it was, too. Surprisingly few Nips visible, apart from those haring around in cars looting. We had to pass some harrowing scenes of casualties lying around on the roadside. One Indian driver, still in the driving seat of his vehicle, had received a direct hit. I shall always remember him, along with all the others who died.

On a triangle of grass where I was dropped off a lorry I had jumped, I was given a swig at a small bottle of champagne. Here began friendship with Henry Hill, a chap who though he drank had, he said, built a church.

Our "home" for the next three months was to be the top floor of C block, Southern Area, Changi. And here begins PoW life.

For kit I had little more than I stood up in. So I started being a vagabond/tinker right early on. I did quite well, being an early bird and having an eye for what might prove useful.

An order came through that all foodstuffs were to be handed in. While demolishing a tin of condensed milk that I had brought from Penang, Colonel Scott of Malacca came by and said "and what the … !" I told him that after carting it through blood, sweat and tears, no one else was going to have it but me. Of the other tins handed in, I saw nothing. However, as many of those who will have enjoyed them are now dead, I can't grumble.

I soon became a magpie. You never saw such an assortment of bits and pieces as was under my tennis-net bed. Captain Fisher of

Fig. 12. Cavalry trumpet (in key F) found in ditch beside road to Changi. Picked it up and sounded "lights out" in barracks at Changi.

our 3rd Battalion, Penang, had found a brass cavalry trumpet, which I lugged to Changi. With the aid of this I installed myself as barrack-block bugler and this excused me sundry fatigues.

The barrack-block area on Changi Point was well designed. In fact it would have been a nice place – grassy slopes, tall trees, paved paths, etc. I am sure the almost cathedral-like effect of those trees and the pleasantness of the surroundings had a deep effect on some of us, certainly on me. With meals consisting of almost invisible rice rations and a few beans (it was seven or eight on one occasion), we found that the senses and aesthetic part of us became sharpened. Tempers were short. But I got great solace from the scenery.

As many of the tutorial staff of Raffles College were there with us, they started quite a little "university". One Shakespearian teacher gave talks with us sitting under a 'spreading chestnut tree' on a grassy bank in the evening, the lovely blue of the sea only spoilt by smoke of burning oil tanks over the Naval Base.

I shall never forget that first Easter Sunday Communion Service, taken by Padre Hall from Penang. We had a small choir, which I had got together. The coolness of the morning, the pillars of the tall trees and the greenness of everything combined to make it most nostalgic, as the university music chap said afterwards.

Rumours, rumours . . . They started very soon. Germany capitulated ten times . . . We shall only be prisoners for a few months . . . The Yanks have landed up the coast. We lived on rumours. Some had no hope and died. Funds were low, though these could only be used on the black market and several operators lost their lives going outside the wire. A change-over onto rice gave me a go of enteritis.

I took to making lamps out of milk tins with a window of mica, plus diesel fuel (see Fig. 13). These went for $2 apiece to officers. Aluminium and sheet rubber sandals at $5. Several nick-nacks I made with new-found patience. I still have an aluminium ring, with inlaid copper wire design of a cross and rays, which took a long time to make (see Fig. 14). There was once an exhibition of handicrafts and some amazing efforts turned up.

Fig. 13. Construction of oil lamp. Cut aperture in tin can using nails
sharpened to chisel. Heating element – wire round mica sheet from smashed
electric toaster. Unwind wire – cut mica to fit window in can. Float with wire
to hold string wick. Fill bottom of can with diesel. I made several for friends.
Changi, Singapore 1942.

One day I returned from a walkabout like a dog with a good
bone. I had lighted upon no less a find than salt. It was that scarce
that we were evaporating sea water. I found a broken wooden box
on a rubbish dump (Fig. 15). With some trepidation I picked up a
white crystal and touched it on my tongue. It was rock salt, four or
five pounds of it. I picked up what I could by hand and took it to

Singapore - Smashed Search light. 1942

Fig. 14. Smashed searchlight. Aluminium circle to hold and protect glass lens. Half moon section. Stripped off chamois leather sheath. Inlaid ring with copper wire using sharpened chisel-shaped nail to cut groove – laid in wire and tamped in. Singapore 1942. The picture to the left shows the ring today.

the cookhouse. The rest I scraped up and put into bottles. Mud sank to the bottom. The solution was welcome on rice. A hungry fellow stroked a cat, grasped it by the tail and it was shortly in the pot.

Except at capitulation I never saw a Nip. Once an inspecting admiral appeared. We had Sikh guards, turncoats who were often drunk. They rarely came inside the wire.

Fig. 15. Small crate on rubbish dump. J.H.R. wandering on look-out found this small wooden crate with white crystals laying around. Tasted and found to be rock salt. With minimal rations – rice – baked beans (six beans to each man). No salt was provided by the Japs. Singapore, Feb/March 1942.

Glen Williams of Raffles ran a good choir. He was quite complimentary to me personally once. We were singing a piece taken from Dvorak's *New World Symphony* and I was to do a solo verse. "Phrasing and tone quite lovely," he said, "actual voice production could be improved."

Working parties began to be called into Singapore. So after a three month stay in Changi, which was not all that unpleasant (barring starvation) I found myself on the march back to Singapore town.

River Valley Road Working Camp, Singapore

In our starved condition it was a wonder that so many of us made it to Singapore town. The Nips had given us a small bag of peanuts as rations for the 15-mile march. A coconut and a drink of cool green Chinese tea helped me make the grade.

We found ourselves in a camp of fifty-odd long atap huts, really quite well spread out, with plenty of room for roll-call and recreation. Double tiers of sleeping platforms. Mates were solicitous, saying that we would soon make ourselves comfortable, as they had. In fact, with our capital, in a very short time our hut was the talk of the camp. Illicit electric light extensions or oil lamps showed quite well furnished bunks, two on each side of each bay. Upstairs bunks were best for privacy.

With filched planks brought in for firewood, Bill Dobbs (ex Swiss ski champion), Molesworth, Noon and I, all of us from Penang, built a two-foot extension, veranda like, lifted the roof on a hinge and made ourselves really comfortable. We had found a ship's heavy brass cabin-lamp. I wish I had it still. Our dining table was on the veranda, leaving plenty of room.

Molesworth was sent back to Changi with suspected diphtheria and Noon was called away in his capacity as Curator of the Waterfall Gardens in Penang. So Bill Dobbs and I, he being bearded by this time, were left alone in luxury. In a ruined building on the "Cabbage Patch" he found two 1 cwt drums of liquid chocolate, a two-gallon drum of condensed milk and drums of essences. I organised the transport of these back to camp on a firewood cart – all to the cookhouse. You should have seen the feast we had. A full-blown curry tiffin of locally purchased materials and then a pudding of ground coconuts soaked in chocolate, with a good layer of condensed milk, and decorations. We had our officer in for tiffin – he got quite a surprise.

Fig. 16. River Valley Road camp. Upper bunk occupied by W. Dobbs and me.
May 1942.

The Cabbage Patch was a swamp area on which we had to build seventeen large godowns (warehouses). For the first two months my party of volunteers, including some Cambridge men, carted literally anything and everything, using the remarkably handy little Nip carts of which there were thousands. The Nips, with whom I got on fairly well, having made an effort with their lingo, treated me very well. In fact I got quite fond of one named Higeta.

Later we were put to work in a saw-mill and the yard around it. It was from here that we got things from the Chinese – the necessaries to run our shops. Bill and I had a small business. He sold tinned goods, I sold peanuts and sweet potatoes, at a small profit for our pains and risk. We had to pay the Chinese a bit, but they also took risks talking to us. A $10 loan from Bill I soon paid off out of profits. It was rather fun. The peanuts were approved by the MO as good against pellagra (cracked skin on scrotum), and other conditions. Other chaps had shops for such things as sewing materials. Our hut was known as change alley – there were no fewer than nine large, well stocked and lit "shops". It was not unknown for Nip soldiers to be found buying things from them.

A nice chapel with plainsong communion services. Major E.W. Swanton (cricket correspondent for the Daily Telegraph) "possessed" and ran an excellent library-hut. I was admitted to his "higher circle" of theological discussion. I gave a lecture there on Church music and also sang in concerts. I was entertainments rep. for our hut and organised lectures, concerts, etc.

Though our first month's labouring seemed eternal, after a bit life became quite bearable. Bags of nails, phosphate and cement all went into the foundations. We had a laugh too, "stocking" the finished godowns with bed bugs.

When the first parties were moved off to the main station, rumour had it that they were for the Cameron Highlands (some hope!). In fact it was for prison trains, with 32 men and more crammed into each metal wagon. In Kuala Lumpur we were allowed to get out to stretch our legs and kip on the platform. Last time I had been through K.L. it was in a first-class carriage! Various stops on the way for benjo. Quite good views of North Malayan jungle, peacocks and jungle birds. Rice chucked into wagons. Red Cross food had arrived too late for us to enjoy it in River Valley Road Camp, but it stood us in good stead on the train. Five days brought us to Bam Pong.

Arrived in Bam Pong, Siam, September 1942. It was under water. The river, which was our saving all the way to Burma, had overflowed. The huts had collapsed. I developed a bad go of Singapore foot, and can thank my lucky stars. Some were marched straight into the jungle. After a few days I was also marched off, but northwards to Nong Pladuk. There I was to be for nine months.

Nong Pladuk, Siam

Entering the main gate in the bamboo fence, in front of me I saw five very long well-built barracks of atap and a wide, hot and dusty area in the open square formed by the huts. All very spacious. The efforts of a Public Works Dept officer made that camp most sanitary and, what was vital, well drained. He had had tons of earth removed.

The general work was unloading sleepers and rails taken from rubber plantations down country. Then loading them on to bogeys to be hauled up the jungle railway. Rails and sleepers were very heavy but we soon got the knack.

The Nips were not unreasonable. We were more-or-less allowed to buy cakes, fruit and, best of all, duck eggs. At first the Thai vendors let us have them quite cheap. Their efforts at English were very funny. Boiled egg = Egcok.

On light duty sick-detail, I was observed to be sharpening a saw by Major Sykes. I had lugged along a small file which I had picked up somewhere. I was promptly incorporated into the permanent building party in the camp. On that delightful job, with no Nips and plenty of spare time, and the pleasant job of hut construction, I remained for five months.

Dear old Major Webb taught me some Urdu. I had choir practices twice a week. At the end we had quite a decent choir. We did both church and secular music, which went down well at concerts. There were lectures. Major Tucker, a big game wallah, was grand. Captains Wilson and Wethey, of Penang, were very decent with their crowd of Indian Army officers. I spent many a pleasant hour with them both in Nong Pladuk and up country.

Some kind individual had abandoned two vital objects – a small bucket and a Hurricane lamp. I "collected" these and pinched diesel for the lamp, and after a little repairing they were OK. Without these two during the next year, I don't know what I should have done, and others had reason to be grateful for them too.

QM Bennett was a character and a mate of mine. He owned a café in Finchley and I promised to look him up.

Latterly, a band used to play working parties out.

Then, at the beginning of the monsoon, I found myself in the pouring rain waiting for a lorry to take me and others up country. Hmm.

Kamburi (Kanchana Buri) July 1943

This is, incidentally, one of the oldest towns in Siam. I have seen it marked as Kanchan Buri on a 17th century map. It was by way of being the HQ for all camps up river to Burma. I was there for four days waiting to go up and join the rail-laying battalion. The party was one hundred strong under dear old Webbo.

Everybody, and particularly one confounded chap called Stonehewer, filled us with horror stories. We knew that we were replacing cholera deaths and other sicknesses, but those people who had already been up country did their best to put the wind up us.

Kinsiok, July 1943

After a day's jolting, the train in which we were jammed, standing, pulled into a deserted siding. It was just dark and the monsoon was doing its stuff. Our tent, if it could be called such, kept a little rain out from above, but a young river flowed merrily through it. In this we slept. One redeeming feature was a surprisingly good meal. Here my little lamp was invaluable, as we were about three quarters of a mile from the cookhouse. One fellow with food got lost and turned up after half an hour. Imagine – Darkness. Rain. Jungle. Mud. A nice welcome to a cholera area. Next day things looked a bit brighter. We put up bamboo sleeping platforms, an activity we got quite good at before long, after many moves.

The following morning at 4.30 a.m. our first rail-laying shift began. No rain-coats or capes, just sacks on our shoulders for carrying sleepers. Captain Veitch of the Northumberland Fusiliers, after driving himself nearly mad with sheets of paper, pouring rain and a hurricane lamp, got the parties sorted out: rail-men, sleeper-men (me), hammer-men, fishplate-men, marker-men ahead using bits of bamboo, etc.

Difficult enough walking across skeleton bridges and doing the contortions necessary to pass feverishly working hammer-men and rail-layers. Practically all the way it was either cuttings or embankments, so there was never much room on the single rail track. One thing that the Nips always allowed was a tea boy, or

Fig. 17. Making Burma Railway. October 1942.

two if we were lucky. They had to move well up ahead to be at the right place for Yasumi (Break) for the chaps laying sleepers and rails. Then they had to up-stakes for a further two or three kilometres and start another fire with wood from a dripping jungle.

Experience of the first shift, when Jonah and I seemed to have carried a very large proportion of the sleepers, showed that a "hancho" (i.e. me as sergeant) with a list of names was essential to prevent men – poor fellows – buzzing off into the jungle for an hour or two. So that was my job: I stood on the rail truck and ticked off the names as the men slid the sleepers off, two to a sleeper.

I confess that I was lucky and thankful for that job. It probably saved me and others something. Who knows! But coming back the next morning, after a nightmare night's work by the light of resin flares, I vomited and diarrhoea-ed and promptly thought my number was up through cholera. It was only a chill, however, not helped by a nasty rash in my groin caused by working twenty-four hours in soaking clothes. Rash disappeared fairly quickly, fortunately, so there was no need to report sick.

Somehow or other the railway progressed, partly, I must admit, due to the ingenuity of the Nips, though they had absolutely no regard for safety – either their own or ours. Now here I must mention the incredible luck of the Nips. Sleepers, bolts, rails would fall off the bridges, accidentally or on purpose, but every time there was a story of near misses on Nips below. This luck, the devil looking after his own, was phenomenal. I have a suspicion that, ironically, the workmanship of the British element helped them a lot.

One thing is generally agreed. No other nationals would have worked with the spirit that we did. The Nips were amazed and actually said so. In particular, our men worked better and sang, even when it was raining, even when myriad jungle midges and mosquitoes bit, even when our evening meal was fourteen hours late and sour when we got it. The same cannot be said of the Dutch or Aussies, I think.

Pram Kasi, August 1943

When the rail was laid well ahead of Kinsiok, up came a tall officer, Colonel Flowers of the Northumberland Fusiliers, to prospect a new camp site. Of course it was raining – pouring – but with much shouting Kinsiok camp was struck. Nip fatigues in this respect were a nuisance as we wanted to see to our own comfort – what little there was to be of it. But the redeeming feature in all this was "perks" nicked from the Nips' cookhouses. I did pretty well.

As is the usual thing in the Army, a few willing horses did all the work, fixing tents and bamboo platforms for everyone's use. Some men are incredibly lazy, or perhaps demoralised and helpless. On looking back though, it was probably just as well that they should get out of the way of those who had any ideas or energy. One chap called Simms, a London bricky (East Surreys), Bidwell, a Norfolk farmer, and I were the "doers" in our section. It was fun and a challenge in a hard way. Jonah, of Coutts Bank, was another good chap, but he "deserted" us for the Nip cook-house. I forgave him when, one miserable day, he came up through mud and rain with what! A leg of chicken fried in a sweetish sauce – a favourite Nip dish. He also won an egg or two from Nip stores, bless him.

F****** Volunteer

One incident did a lot to encourage me. I held the rank of sergeant in the SSVF. It was known that I was not a regular. Nevertheless, Gunso/Sarge I was, and had quite a bit of responsibility. Having a little Japanese, I had often to speak for the men and also had to relay orders from the Nip engineers.

So there we were, back in camp. I had carried this small bucket all along. We soon learnt that it was essential to have something, mug or tin or some container, to collect anything that might be going – rice, water, tea, and even diesel leaking from a rail engine. One time my bucket went missing. I found it eventually – it had been borrowed by a rather demoralised young serviceman who used it to boil his duck eggs. We could buy these from Siamese boat men on the river, our pay, if we got it, being about half a Tical a day (i.e. half a rupee, one shilling). Anyway, I gave this young chap a piece of my mind. I wouldn't have used the bucket for cooking and he had no ******* right to do so. Whereupon he gave me a whole lot of lip. At this point Lance Corporal Jackie Ayres and his mate, both regulars of East Surrey Regiment, took this chap outside and gave him what for. "You b***** well do what Sarge says, or else!" All of which did a lot for my standing as sergeant. I was grateful.

By this time beriberi was setting in, and as this affects both body and mind one must not blame people. Thank God I was still quite fit.

The River Kwa Noy (The Main River)

Remember, the railway ran of necessity up the river, and I must say again what a mercy that river was in many ways. Barges navigated by Siamese brought food up the river, took sick men down, brought irregular canteen supplies – sticky gula Malacca (sugar), peanuts, fags of indescribable Thai tobacco. We bathed in the river, and the cookhouse relied on it too.

I have never been so desolate as at dusk one day in rain in jungle far from camp. No shelter or food, with a night's work ahead of me. Just murky fungoid greenery in profusion. Utterly inhospitable.

One night-shift on the embankment the conditions were pretty frightful – full monsoon, lightning and heaven knows what. Dripping jungle, damp and miserable, having to lug those sleepers on the limited space beside the rail bogeys. When all of a sudden into this grotty situation comes up the voice of Jackie Ayres. Jackie had been a barrow boy, and something, somebody, put it into his head to call out very loud "All ripe and loverlee! take yer baby's arse orf the barrow-o! pissed all over the strawberries-ees!" Silence! Then a roar of applause, for all that the men were exhausted. He cheered everyone up with the sheer cheek of it, as well as the sound of home. Nips went mad, of course. Kurrah! Dammedaro! But they needn't have worried. No spare energy there.

Sleepers

In breaks from work due to non-arrival of rail and sleeper trains, far the best place to sleep was on a sleeper. It was only wet. I put in some surprisingly good winks on them. Why no one got rheumatism I don't know. All medical rules and peace-time warnings went by the board and we seemed to get away with it mostly. Extraordinary operations, people recovering from cholera under vile conditions (a few only), and as for fevers – everybody had them, but had perforce to ignore them. The low cholera figure in Flossie's group was a credit to his zeal. Boil, boil, boil! Everything! At first it seemed an impossibility to carry out all Flossie's orders on this score, but fortunately bamboo burns well and there was plenty of that, and he taught us all the art of fire-making. Instead of the usual to-do, we soon got used to assessing how much wood was necessary for a particular boiling. A fire was lit and out in quite a short space. Incidentally, Flossie was our rather irreverent name for Colonel Flowers of the Northumberland Fusiliers. He did survive, I am very glad to say.

The weather improved and the work seemed to get lighter. I spent many a relatively pleasant evening in the officer's tent with Wilson, Wethey and other Indian Army officers. Why, we even had cigars of a sort, and coffee. Pretended that they were real, as in better times. Quite merry!

Cowcatchers and Rustlers

We had just finished laying a trainload of sleepers and rails. We were wondering what to do until the next lot arrived when a lone calf was spotted in the distance. I was well in the vanguard of the chase that followed, visualising a nice steak. After a lot of different tactics the calf took to water. It was felled by a spiking hammer, its throat cut with my ever present and ever useful jack-knife. I am sorry to say that later a very worried Dutchman appeared out of the rainy gloom enquiring politely for a calf. No one said anything, but a half oil drum was emitting the most sumptuous smells. Too bad – poor old Dutchman.

A Good Word for Once

The Nips of this party were all engineers and N.C.O.s. They were a cut above the slave-driving type, and soon realised that force was the last thing to use if they wanted their precious railway built. Once I was left by myself with six men, jacks, crowbars and spirit level, for a fortnight. Just levelling and straightening a big siding. It was really rather delightful. Our engine-driver corporal played draughts with the siding-keeper all day. A pleasant, deep spoken, considerate fellow.

Tamajo

Our first view of what in the end became a very fair camp site was a well-watered paddy field. Here we arrived after a four-kilometre hike carrying dripping atap in the rain. The original site in that area was cholera-contaminated and unusable. From this site we finished the railway up to the Burma border.

The rains had let up a bit and the work eased owing to the

length of line behind us. A dry 24-hour shift was relatively enjoy-able, being able to keep one's balance without slipping, often down a steep embankment with a heavy sleeper following one. The Nips were pleased and coughed up quite a decent cigarette "presento". There was no regular issue. We could spend our 25 cts a day on duck eggs and gula Malacca and limes.

When I say the rail was finished, it was the actual rails that were connected with those laid by the Aussies up through Burma. The sleepers had yet to be inserted as latterly they only put five or six sleepers under each rail. The most boring job was ballasting. As for ballast, it came from the granite in the hills. In teams of three we had one chap holding the chisel and two with hammers. We had to drill three 30 cm holes per day, per three men. Nips did the blasting, of course.

So there we were, perched up on perilous rock some 80 to 100 feet above the rail. The river was below, dear old river. I saw then, with some awe, the first heavy engine crawl up the track. It was the second shift, not mine, which had the pleasure of actually joining the rails. The moment was not without pride. Regardless of how, we had after all helped build the bally thing. Needless to say, there was a typical Nip ceremony with brass band.

Returning by rail to camp in the early morning after this final shift, one was naturally tired. There was no such thing as sitting room on these open trucks. As far as I know only one bloke fell off through going to sleep, and he fell into a pond. He was rescued by a Chinese whom he had pulled off with him. The Chinese showed real modesty when he mingled with the rest of his gang and could not be traced. I never quite fell off. But on several occasions I saw ghosts of PoWs trudging up and down the irregular path on the packed earth beside the track. I remember how I distinctly saw them wearing the wide-brimmed straw hat, a Dutch army issue which most of us had acquired. The ghosts would disappear, merg-ing into bushes as I came nearer. Then I would pinch or shake myself, as I knew I should soon fall off.

The most dreaded part of that or any other journey was "all men pushee". The diesel engine could not grip the wet rails on anything like an incline. The cry would go up. Nobody would move. Tired out as we were, we hoped some sucker would jump out. Then along would come a Nip with a long bamboo, wielding it with both hands. It was a disadvantage to be tall when that was happening.

Woodcutting

At this camp we stayed put, felling trees for firewood for the engines. Facing the Jungle, this was the task: per party of ten men, with two cross-cut saws, an axe and a wedge, to produce one stack of 50 cm split logs, 1 metre by 5 metres, per day. At first this was difficult, but we soon got to know which trees split easily when felled – in fact we got quite expert. On this job – for once – the Nips kept their promise and, their task done, a gang was allowed to set off for camp quite alone.

From the botanical point of view this was a most interesting job. The monsoon was over and the jungle made an effort to produce a flower or two – very few. The fungi were most interesting; luminous ones stuck in our hats one very dark night were quite a sight. There was a small creeping plant growing on the banks of the river. It was a kind of purslane and quite edible. Urine is quite a good fertiliser, so a few of us were to oblige. This was the sort of tip that the Indonesian soldiers passed on to us. Vitamin C is the one to stave off beriberi. I found some shrimps in a fresh water pool by a cascade. They went red when boiled and were tasteless. And I vowed, as we often did, that we would catch up on shrimps and suchlike, eating with a vengeance, when free!

Here I got my first fever, to be followed by jaundice and what was perhaps black water fever.

Captain Ian Wethey

At this point Ian came to my rescue. He had been introduced to me by the Syer family at the swimming club in Penang. Always of modest bearing, except in rugger when he thoroughly enjoyed himself. He sang quietly but tunefully in the carol choir. One morning as I was washing out my tin in the river, he came up to me rather shyly, saying that he was sorry I was having such a rotten time. Would I be insulted with a ten Tical note? I took the ten Ticals gladly and appreciatively. They were invested entirely in brown sugar. On this, with a little rice and very poor "gippo" off the meagre vegetable ration, I lived for three weeks, jaundice untreated. Ian's ten Ticals and some limes he brought me in fact kept me alive.

Major Leighs

I never knew him personally, but my "Good morning, Sir" was always very honestly replied to. A real Scottish laird, even in frayed khaki. So imagine what the Nips thought when greeted with the sight of Major Leighs in highland dress, in the mud of a jungle camp on a Sunday! A grand sight.

He and the congregation were once obliged to smack each other's faces for singing the National Anthem after a service. On parade one day some Thais walked between him and his parade. "What the devil do you mean by breaking the ranks of British soldiers, damn you!" I don't suppose the startled Thais understood him, but they were more or less blown away by his vehemence.

Captain Elton

I can't remember when I first met Captain Elton of the Indian Army and started what to me was a valuable friendship, which I hope was reciprocated. I think it may have been in Webbo's Urdu class in Nong Pladuk. He was jolly decent in interest and also in small presents. Many a pleasant evening we had. I was sorry to leave him in Nong Pladuk 2 on the way to Japan, and sorry to leave Webbo too. The last thing Elton did was to carry my kit as I was dashing after some last minute canteen stuff for the blokes.

I pray that these people are well. I must in all conscience try to do something to show my gratitude to them. In a quiet way they were sympathetic to me and to other volunteer rankers. It was not always easy living at such close quarters with all and sundry all the time, though I learnt much from them and grew to like some very much, particularly Simms and Bidwell.

In August 1943 I got letters. Six in all, from Mother, Father and Betty. All these were written a year before, in August and September 1942. They were absolute bliss to receive. At intervals we had been given printed cards to fill in – about eight in all. How many got through, I wonder?

Hindato, November 1943

It was unfortunate that the move to this camp took place on a very cold night. All mist and moonlight. I was feverish and bilious but had to ignore it and fight for myself, carrying my rather heavy kit three kilometres that end. I even raised the energy to make a cup of tea before retiring under a canvas rag called a tent. Result – four days semi-delirious. Medical attention nil. Jonah got me food, but I ate little and produced much bile. I was not at all happy and just didn't care. Lowest ebb.

Against all probability I was about again after a week. I found myself in a very pleasant camp under cool jungle trees on a plateau above the river. The river here was really beautiful, with an excellent beach for swimming. Unfortunately I found the climb down and up again too much for me at first. One memorable day we were paraded on the bank of the river, ready to dive in. A Nip went up stream a bit and threw in a hand grenade. Masses of stunned fish floated up and the chaps had to go in and get them. Everyone did well out of that.

Christmas 1943

A large and enthusiastic choir under Mr Purcell of the Northumberland Fusiliers went carol singing by the light of pitch flares. I was told that it was "charming" and most true to home style. Imagine the ruddy flicker of torches on pillar-like jungle trees behind intent faces.

Really a jolly Christmas in spite of all. One Nip, old Cheetah, even walked through our huts saying Happy Christmas. Not a bad old boy really. He was mad on decorated gardens – so much so that we got rather fed up with them.

Don't tell me it was over-eating – an impossibility – but I spent the next three weeks in the hospital hut with colitis. The doctor was an Anglo Indian and did an excellent job in that hospital.

Books

I am a very slow reader. Unless I consider a book instructive I can't be bothered with it. Perhaps to a fault, I absorb completely whatever I *do* read. While in hospital at Hindato, Elton got me *The Days of our Years* by Peter Parsons, which I thoroughly enjoyed; it lasted me three weeks. Then *Heloise and Abelard* lasted nearly as long. Elton also got me *The Last of the Empresses*, which I found vitally interesting at Tamajo, again in hospital.

In Japan I had Marie Corelli's *Ardath*. This impressed me more than any book I have read. In fact, it plumbed me to the roots and made things religious much more concrete for me.

The Last Puritan, which dear old Casey (yet to be introduced) got me, was very interesting. Beyond these, apart from *The Jungle Book*, which I had back in River Valley Road camp in Singapore, and of course the Bible, I can't remember reading anything worthwhile. But then I am a doer, thank God.

Hindato (Again)

You would have been alarmed at my appearance when I emerged from hospital there. Scarecrow wasn't in it! Wethey was very helpful again in approaching one Colonel Hartigan. They got me a job in the canteen then being built and I worked under quite congenial conditions for most of the next two months. There were advantages in being behind the counter, as it were. It did a lot to build me up. But I am sure that, as before, it was the mental ease of having no Nips in charge of me that was more healing than anything.

Jonah, a fellow Volunteer, and I alternated fevers conveniently at this time, so we were able to care for each other. He had a job in the cookhouse, so he and I were well set up and made ourselves quite comfortable in the long atap hut. The eaves of this type of hut reached to the ground, a new style but not very waterproof – what were a few drops of rain to us, though!

The River Kwa Noy

I must stress again the beauty of the river here. The whistle of the gibbon monkeys was quite cheerful. Their whooping and wailing echoed through the creeper-decked jungle giants across the river in the early mornings.

On the Move

Now started a move down country at last. Although half and more of the camp had already left for base at Nong Pladuk, full rations were still being delivered and we lived in a bit of a dream with more meat pasties than we could eat and pints of stew. We could help ourselves to sweet potatoes and pumpkins. My little pot and Jonah's frying pan again came into their own and we did wonders with the ever welcome gula. I should like to get some gula Malacca home and show off its possibilities. The four-gallon tins were used again and again for every purpose imaginable – cooking ovens, wash buckets, dustpans, showers, etc. etc. I will go so far as to say that if there had been no four-gallon tins there would have been no railway.

Hindato hadn't been all that bad, especially our last ten days there, although there was a high fever incidence and sadly several cases of fatal cerebral malaria. It was here in Hindato that we heard the joyful sound of our planes overhead quite regularly. The Nips went mad every time. Funny!

Ngong Pladuk No. 2, March 1944

Travelling down on our own railway was quite a thing. "We did this bit, . . . did that bit." And then Pram Kasi. One could see very clearly how the building of a railway can open up a countryside. Of course it was all military stuff, but Pram Kasi was unrecognisable even after only four months.

A lot of jungle had been cleared by coolies, who lived in tents up the side of a hill. When we knew it, the area had been covered with jungle creeper. When this creeper gets a hold it devastates large areas of jungle. Now it looked as though it had been war-blasted and then invaded by the creeper. The effect of this was quite haunting, particularly at dusk. Very inhospitable in rain.

Down from the mountainous region of the Three Pagoda Pass the countryside flattens out and the rail passes through flat wide plains with paddy fields. I must say that I was glad to see something other than perpetual jungle at short range, or where the line ran high above the river on some rocky ledge, with jagged and inhospitable bare mountains across a valley.

At Ngong Pladuk, when we got there, we were in tents until we had built our own huts. These were of improved design and really quite respectable. Everything was much more expensive than when we were last down country – prices had risen with increasing populations of Nips, Malays and Chinese. Quite a good canteen was run by our "friends" among the Dutch. Actually we were not very friendly. The "native" element was rather a rub with prisoners as a whole, though I must say that the few Dutchmen whom I had in my choir at Nong Pladuk No. 1 were excellent fellows. I got to understand them and to like their serious (possibly rather unimaginative) attitude to life.

I was no good to man or beast in this camp, as like many others I would have fever for five days, get over it in one or two more, and by the fifth day again I would have another go of fever. At least I was able to read. Food did not interest me much, though an occasional "Sambal Bajak", the famous Dutch product at 10 cts a portion, went down well. I, of course, was not getting any pay (25 cts a day) and here again Elton was jolly decent. And there were bananas, good old gula Malacca sugar, and duck eggs (always duck eggs, never chicken's, duck eggs being about the size of a decent English hen's egg and chicken's eggs like a moorhen's effort). Soya-bean cakes brightened life a bit.

This was the biggest camp I had been in since Changi. The size of the camp had its advantages and one could move around visiting a bit. As far as I was concerned, work was always inside the camp – construction work and drain digging. So apart from the blistering heat and fever coming and going, it wasn't too bad, and we liked the regular hours.

Koreans

I have not said anything about these unfortunates. We grew to hate them even more than the Nips. It was typical of Nip mentality to put captives – Koreans were little more than that – in charge of captives. Needless to say the Koreans got their own back on us. For none of which were they to be blamed – the Nips were entirely responsible for their condition. All that didn't console us much, though. As a rule apparently the camp administration was done by Koreans. We reckoned that the Nips wouldn't trust them as proper soldiers. But stealing PoW rations was a foregone conclusion. This was most noticeable later on the 28-day ship journey to Japan. It was shocking. May all Koreans return to their farms in Korea and stay there.

Friendly Planes

At the sound of any planes, even though quite invisible, some anti-aircraft gunners just over the camp fence would open up. That was altogether fun. The sound of the planes was tremendously heartening, as it had been back in Hindato. B29 bombers were just rumours to us – they were planes of fabulous size! One cook swore that he saw a plane pass the moon one night. It was a colossal thing and obscured the moon for minutes! The sound was most musical at night as we lay in our huts. Needless to say there was pandemonium among the Japs. But one needed to be careful still.

Low Ebb

From Nong Pladuk 2 there went every day a detail known as the "ammo party". In trucks we jolted along past Nong Pladuk 1, our old home, and then out across flat paddy fields for about 5 miles. Under mango trees, over quite a large area, were dotted camouflaged, well built sheds full of ammunition. Our job was to dig an eight-foot trench around the perimeter of this area. It was a combination of things that went together to depress my optimism down to a nasty low in this place. Fever of course didn't help, but the efficiency of the running of the ammunition dump, and something in the very contrast between the peaceful setting of tall, cool mango trees and what they hid, depressed me badly. Things seemed to be going all too well for the Nips. The weather was lovely; the countryside very attractive; temple gongs sounding and saffron robed monks around. The awful truth of captivity, with very little hope, was shattering. Even the blooming rumours were not too good.

Roll Call – Tengko!

Normally twice a day, these roll calls were sometimes quite funny. Sometimes not at all so. At Changi we were not bothered much; not so up in Thailand. But I don't suppose the Nips knew or cared how many had died since last roll call.

Back in River Valley Road camp the whole performance had been quite a friendly affair. For a lark we would number as a pack of cards (Jack, Queen, King). We had been obliged to learn Nip drill, including their complicated "about turn". Also by this time we were supposed to be able to number in Nip (ichi, ni, san, shi, go). Some never would or could! At first they did not keep us hanging about, but we soon made up for it in Nong Pladuk 2. Two hours as often as not, morning and evening, to say nothing of periodical surprise searching. Then everyone, fever or not, was turned out unceremoniously to sit in the boiling sun for three or four hours. Those searches gave rise to much cruelty and punishment. Horrible Kempetai (military police)!

Japanwards

At first the rumours had it that the big sorting-out into units was preparatory to going up country again for maintenance work and bomb repairs. That sent shivers down my spine. My ingenuity and energy had been sufficient to help me through one go up country, but malaria had sapped most of it by now.

My fears, in that direction anyway, were quieted when, in a torrential downpour, having said some sad goodbyes to Elton, Webb, Wethey and others, I found myself headed for the station. Cattle trucks again. I promptly threw a terrific fever that lasted three days or so, so I wasn't interested in anything much. Two more days and I was able to take in the scenery. That is when it was my turn "at the door". Goods wagons had sliding doors and the doors had to have space in which to slide. That's all right if the wagon is not so tightly packed as to leave no room for the door to slide. Cause of a lot of trouble as there was hardly room for many to lie out flat.

Travelling down through southern Siam, into Malaya through Pahang and Selangor, all of which were familiar to me, was upsetting. I could just see Penang over the sea. Then past Kuala Lumpur and the swimming club, all in enemy hands. I had lived in the Station Hotel at K.L.

River Valley Road Camp – Again!

Our party was under the care of 2nd Lieutenant Orrocks, with whom I became very intimate. A quiet, god-fearing Scot who did a thoroughly praiseworthy job under most difficult conditions for discipline. There was no form of punishment, such as being put on a charge, among us prisoners. We owe much to his understanding and sacrifice of his own pride. Nothing spectacular either for good or bad under his rule – far the best thing in the long run. For diligence in holding prayer meetings back in Thailand and later in Japan he deserves the highest praise.

We stayed only one night in River Valley Road. During that time Orrocks and I had a fine old time sorting out some fantastically priced canteen stores which were thrown at us – some horrible "cakes" were meant to be a treat, but cost two days' pay and took only a minute to eat! The accounts kept him busy all the way to Japan.

We had time to observe some Indian PoWs there, though we were not supposed to fraternise. They had been working in

Singapore, or Shonanto as the Nips re-named it, and seemed pretty well off to me. I was impressed by the jolly temple they had got rigged up, with brightly illuminated pictures of Siva and Krishna and various objects of veneration in proper Hindu style. Cantor chanting away in plainsong-like monotone which I found very acceptable.

Next morning we were on the march – this time to the docks. There we boarded No. 8 in the convoy.

Prison Ship ***** *Maru* to Japan

So, on 1st June – Dad's birthday, as I remembered rather ruefully – we found ourselves being squeezed and "more squeezed" into the cargo compartment under the bridge structure of a 6000 ton cargo ship. This ship was what I should call badly overloaded with iron ore; so much so that there was only about seven feet of freeboard just forward of the bridge where the gunwale sloped down away from the bows – we knew all about this later. Roped onto the outside of the rails were a number of precarious looking wooden Benjo contraptions for the call of nature, delivering straight into the sea below. Up forward on the port side was the cookhouse structure.

Well, it was the nearest approach to the Black Hole of Calcutta that I ever hope to be involved in. Having been crammed into the space under the bridge structure we had to sort ourselves out on the wooden platforms used, I suppose, for deck cargoes. Only two doors to the outside.

I soon began another go of malaria. For the best part of a month our diet was rice, dried fish and roots of some sort. I couldn't eat much of that. One of our chaps from Malaya was glad enough to go and get my rations, and eat what I couldn't. Two wooden tanks (a pet idea of the Nips) were filled with fresh water each day by an old Nip deck hand who was quite friendly to us.

I was in a dazed state for much of the time and was quite content to lie inside the "black hole" and out of the painful glare of the sun, just opening one eye to dwell on that godsend of a book *The Daily Telegraph Miscellany*. This was lent to me by a very good friend, Arthur Silk, and saw me through nearly the whole voyage.

In my army pack I had a few bits and pieces – some things I had made including the aluminium ring, clothing, my razor and a little glass hone to sharpen it. I had also carried a small tin of Marmite all this time, against emergencies. This was one. So I got the tin open and made it last – it probably saved my bacon.

And so I lay there, not caring much about anything – food, depth charges, torpedoes or, I am afraid, other ships being sunk. Others, I think, must have been in a frightful state of mind knowing they were in a death trap.

I used to creep outside on deck at dusk and night time, when the glare would have abated. Had a good look at Taiwan and also Manila Bay. An excellent harbour in Taiwan, hills all round except a narrow entrance. A few quite nice-looking houses, probably for officials. Otherwise the usual Japanese/Chinese hovels seemingly made of anything from the salvage line on shore. A lot of shipping and warships hiding from Yank subs. It was in Manila Bay that a Filipino stevedore had it that these waters were alive with subs. Certainly the four destroyers escorting us dropped a lot of depth charges, which shook our boat.

As we got nearer Japan it got colder and rougher. Men stayed outside as long as they were allowed, braving spray and rain. The sea began to come over the sides and we had to have every man on the doors to bang them shut every time a wave threatened. How the bang of that door banged through my head! I once saw a green wall of water fill the door. Everything got wet and stayed wet.

At last we arrived at a very dull looking place where we were told we should get off. A sigh of relief went up. This was Moji, Honshu, Japan. As we wound up a creek, eventually a fine harbour, packed with shipping, opened out before us.

Japan: Moji to Funatsu

Quite unceremoniously and without any warning we were counted off like so many cattle as we stood on the quayside. As a result many chums got separated. In a life where one had so little, one's chums were one's greatest asset – much more than ever before – so this herding apart struck hard on many people.

It was a joyful moment when we saw the Koreans go off in a lorry in the opposite direction to us – we were glad to see the back of them.

The Nips here were really much more civil than the ones we had known before. There was one English-speaking Jap who did what he could for us and was very civil to Orrocks, our officer. Some young Nip guards eyed us askance as we sat waiting and eating cold fish and rice hash out of all sorts of receptacles. I think they were surprised that we were so subdued.

It was on the ferry across the harbour to the station that I saw, after all those years, the first "unnecessary" decorations. Just a ceiling light with green and white glass, and then green velvet sprung seats. You can guess what a surge of regret/envy/something arose in me – what a reminder of home! But also a dull reminder of the fact that we were now beyond all rescue or escape. We were now right in the lion's den.

On the train we had to travel three men to a "two" seat, a short Nip seat at that. We didn't have much room for our long thin legs. We got quite a good view of the super-intense cultivation of every inch of ground. There were few roads to be seen, mostly narrow tracks; that was all they could spare. This seemed to be sufficient, as old men and old women were all we saw in the countryside. When the train came opposite any naval or military objects, down would go the blinds. This was not confined to PoWs, but even Nip troops had to conform. Needless to say people peeped on both sides, and on one or two occasions the look was far from hostile or anything but interested.

Our food came in neat little boxes made of the ever-useful pine wood. One little box, 5 × 4 × 1 inch, of rice with a patriotic red cherry in the middle, another little box with salty pickled veg. and two kinds of seaweed in compartments; chopsticks thrown in. Of course, we were being treated, at last and for the only time, as "troops of the country of capture" (Geneva Convention).

Osaka

More little boxes as, in the early hours of the morning of 26th June, we squatted in the covered roadway outside Osaka station. They made us sit facing inwards so the curious populace should not see how much we were getting. As for us, the knickerbocker suits and kimonos were thrilling to see, insofar as anyone had any thrill-ability left.

I kicked myself out of lethargy and told myself to sit up and take notice of Japan, in what I hoped were her death throes. Empty, mocking shop windows; tottering little men in knee breeches and boaters; cattle yards full of very young Nip soldiers waiting to be shipped for slaughter.

I mustn't forget. Back in Thailand we had been given one set of new British clothing. This we were ordered to wear while travelling. And forsooth, though we still presented a pretty queer spectacle, if they had not given us that kit many of us would have been indecently dressed for a city. It had hardly mattered in the jungle.

The Journey In

The train organisation is undoubtedly first class in Japan. Trains would flash back and forth at high speed incredibly frequently. Girls operating point levers would first stand in front of the desired lever, bow to it, and then pull. After a considerable time climbing, winding in and out of tunnels, along rocky ledges, over torrents below, past modern-looking power stations and pylons in most inaccessible places, we eventually saw snow high away in the distant mountains. Little did we realise that was our destination.

At Gifu we finally changed onto a mountain mining railway.

Not carriages but bogies designed for carrying zinc ingots, and now four men to an open bogey. Careful instructions about dangling legs and height of heads. We visualised all sorts of tunnels and mines, and were proved right. Quite surprisingly we were fortified with a couple of rice balls each. Only one old man muttered away at us as we passed through a small mining town. It was night and we were getting colder every minute.

Funatsu Prison Camp

I could hardly walk from the train at Funatsu what with jolt numbness and cramp and cold. But in pitch blackness we did walk, hugging the wall by order, along a precipitous path to the camp, which path we were soon to know all too well.

The camp was surrounded by a wooden fence with ridiculous wooden spikes. A typical Nip effort. It was more to show people outside that it was a prison camp than to keep us in. At first I laughed at the spikes. Later, when spirits were low, they had a depressing effect. Anyhow, thousands of feet up a mountain valley, how could one escape? Up this chasm came everything. The mountain railway wound round steep mountains on either side, pretty well into the centre of Japan (Honshu).

The camp consisted of two two-storey billets and sundry smaller buildings. Everything was made of wood, even the roof tiles. The billets were brand new. The straw matting on the bed spaces tacked down over loose straw was clean and reasonably comfortable. We were amazed to find five blankets per man. More about these blankets later. At the time it seemed positive luxury, though knowing the Nips' "generosity" it did not bode too well for the temperature in the future. The sun shone, for the short time that it was clear of the mountains on either side, and the sky was blue and clear, but even in midsummer there was a nip in the air out of the sun.

For the first few days we were taken for runs, walks and PT, organised by Casey Hoyle. About this time of the year there was growing everywhere a weed which gave off a sort of laundry smell;

Fig. 18. Funatsu Prison Camp 3000/4000 feet. Reached by light railway. Everything – stores, equipment, zinc ingots, prisoners, etc. travelled on short four-wheel bogeys. Four men on a bogey. One had to hold tight.

this was not unpleasant in itself, but I grew to hate it, with its association. About four days after our arrival, when the food was plentiful if unvaried, we were compelled to write a letter of our impressions. But, Nip-like, when they had got our letters the food went down with a bang. And so it stayed until the end. The one exception was at Christmas when we received the first Red Cross parcel – the one and only.

We had all progressively lost weight and, of course, any layer of fat, and bitterly cold months lay ahead of us. I never had a full belly again. I got another fever soon. Given the thumping headache and shivering, and thankfully not being compelled to work in spite of fever, it was possible to be quite philosophical and just sweat it out.

PoW Labour – the Factory, June 1944

We were told airily that we should be working – some of us in mines, some in factories – according to our abilities. Orrocks had the peculiar task of sorting out "intelligences". The clever ones, including volunteers, were to go into the zinc electrolysis and smelting factory. Others had to break up ore with heavy hammers, others to work in the acid plant, others in the lead smelting plant. The ores of these metals were mined out of the hill facing us by the Dutch PoWs whose billets we could see up the hill. Rumour had it that gold, silver and other metals were present in small quantities as well.

After a bit we were sent to the factory, the Ion Denkai. The sole product was zinc. Zinc in the form of ingots 30 × 15 × 3 cm.

Fig. 19. German-built zinc smelting factory on steep mountainside near village of Funatsu, rail head of light railway. Here are piles of sheet zinc yet to be smelted. Electric induction furnaces, see moulds in the front/below furnace, piles of ingots. One ingot inset – E M C on ingot stands for Electrical Matsui Company. 1944/45.

They had the letters E M C on each one – Electric Mitsui Company. At least, I think that is what they stood for. The factory was of German design and the zinc could have been for export in better times. The construction of the very considerable building was varied. Looking down from a height it was of cathedral-like appearance. It was quite inspiring to walk along the flying walkways at the top and look down through many metres of pillars and arches. The eye moved past great Wellsian revolving drums and again into vast vats of devilish-looking brews bubbling and steaming.

Far down to my right would be PoWs working in high rubber boots knee deep in sludge and darkness and acid fumes. I being a so-called technical person was above mere digging, but the chaps

Fig. 20. Zinc ore brought on bogeys from mountainside. Mixed with sulphuric acid in vats – some settling. Fluid passed through filter cloths (very useful to prisoners for other purposes). Fluid piped into electric vats with steel plates upon which zinc is deposited by electrolysis. Sheets stripped off steel sent through to furnaces for smelting. 1944/45.

said it wasn't too bad. Further down were the vats, two metres long and a metre deep, where the acid (plus zinc) was piped after being filtered. Incidentally, when the filter cloth was discarded, it could be washed and pummelled till it became quite soft; it had many uses, including gloves and balaclavas. These vats had suspended into them steel sheets with lugs on them. Electric hoists were there to lift them out. Zinc was deposited by electrolysis onto both sides of the steel sheets and the zinc was stripped off with a flat tool. Each batch took about 18 hours to be completed. The wet zinc sheets were wheeled through to the Denkillo (furnace department). Owing to the deterioration of some during processing, the zinc sheets came in all sorts of conditions – some thick and difficult to bend, some knobbly, some thin and brittle. The sheets had to be folded in order to get them into the mouth of the five furnaces, fed from the open top and stirred with a wooden paddle. Woe betide anyone if a sheet should be too moist: pouff, and molten zinc was everywhere. If there was a blow-out, molten zinc and clouds of brown dross would fly everywhere, right up to the ceiling rafters, and everyone would take cover before it had time to come down again. When the smoke had cleared, the stoker might be all right, or very much not all right.

After working for a bit in the electrolysis vats I was promoted to the Denkillo (furnaces) and given an armband! Now an armband to the Nip mentality was a great thing. It means you are somebody. There was I – it was plain for all to see – Hancho of the Denkillo on our shift.

The Pour Out

When the level of zinc was up, everyone would get ready for the fun. Electricity off at the transformer. One man ready at the tilting wheel, another with a spike ready to pierce the bung-hole half way down the furnace side. Another man standing ready by the half circle of moulds, armed with a piece of wood to ward off the molten zinc as it flowed down the chute. In his other hand he had the bent handle attached to the chute and had to direct the flow into the moulds – thirteen of them. Theoretically this gave time for the first mould to set. But another chap had to be ready with a bucket of water to cool things down. Hopefully the insides of the ingot would not ooze out on the platform when the trigger was pulled to tip the mould out. The chap on the chute had to waltz round double quick to the beginning. Someone else would rake out ingots from underneath and gingerly pick them up with plenty of old gloves and stack them.

I used to like the pouring out, though many were a little scared of the job. One certainly had to look slippy. I had many a hole burnt in my clothing and rubber shoes. I was often ordered to do this although I was supposed to be a non-working Hancho. But one got quite a kick out of seeing handsome ingots, and the molten metal itself was fascinating. In mid-winter it was also warm work. The big transformers made a deep humming noise. I would idly imagine the zinc to be the boiling of primordial masses of quicksilver. One entered into quite a reverie with the spectrum of colours on the surface of clean zinc.

I had to take a turn at two scary jobs. Bucketing sludge up out of a mixing vat – quite a small hole in the top and a metal ladder down inside, with three of us straddling the lead paddles. There was quite a resonance when nearly empty. I got us singing "London's Burning" as a round. A face looked down through the hole, but said nothing. Another time inside the fire box of a boiler, chipping away the hard coating of white deposit with a small sharp hammer, I was peeping at my New Testament by the light of an inspection lamp. This time I did get called out to face an officer. Strangely, nothing happened when I showed them the N.T., nor did they take it away.

Some Nip Characters

The head Hancho of our shift was named Burias San. A small, thin, though fine man with slanting eyes. A craftsman, and so good a foreman that men called him the Wolf. He always seemed to be watching them quietly from some corner. He was always quiet and never hit anyone. He never spoke to anyone except through me. It was not long before we understood each other fairly well. And, believe it or not, one day I found myself giving him a brief outline of early English history. He was keen to learn English and had an amazing memory. He liked to get hold of long, abstruse words and use them quaintly. One Nip described the oriental mind as a spiral anticlockwise and the western mind as clockwise (hence a whole lot of misunderstanding).

Unlike Burias, Hashimoto San was not at all educated in anything artistic. It was a long time before I got on with him at all. He would suddenly leap out of his room, round up his men and any odd PoW who didn't look too busy. He would whirl them off in a frenzy to move a mountain of dirt or accumulated dross. He would go quite mad, but did get the stuff moved in a very short time. Others had left it or looked at it for weeks. Typical way of getting things done Nip-wise. He was called "the whirlwind", a pop-eyed, rude-mouthed, uncultured ex-army man.

Yasumi, or Yazmy

One thing the Nips were keen on throughout all our PoW experience was Yazmy – rest. I was pleasantly surprised at this early on when putting wheels on handcarts back in Singapore. Drop everything. And the more fool you if you didn't. Conscientiousness, to the extent of working one minute after the Yazmy bugle, whistle, flag or shout had gone up, was not appreciated at all.

I saw the reason for this after a bit in Japan. The poor devils didn't know what Sunday or holiday meant. Work was work, and for the most part unpleasant. That is, if it were done as it was meant to be, or when any big-shot was about. I will say this too, that whenever possible they would provide tea or allow us to fix our own. In the jungle in Thailand this was sometimes an impossibility, though, as I wrote earlier, it's amazing what can be done even in a dripping wet jungle. Tricks of the trade learned the hard way.

The Rest Room – Ion Denkai

We started work in the summer months, of course. The Rest Room, where I for one stretched my weary "beriberi" legs for just as long as possible during Yazmys, had been newly boarded off from the factory. In the course of the months our poor old undernourished muscles got used to the labour. Then it began to get cold and the rest room came into its own. I am afraid that the selfishness of some men stretching full length meant that the latecomers could not get comfortable – the reason was that I and my Denkillo men got later and shorter Yazmys than the supposedly harder working Denkai men. I therefore used to retire underneath one of the furnaces, wrapped up in my British Army great coat. That the furnace was part-filled with molten zinc, and sputtered every now and then, made me feel a little warmer.

Steam pipes in various places were used for cleaning and other purposes, and there was one under the end furnace where I used to kip. Outside the factory was a canteen, where everything was supplied by the company. I spotted some vegetable tops which had been thrown out of a window and collected some of them, put them in my billy can and turned on the steam – they actually tasted quite good.

I also did a little private casting. The furnaces were lined with a specialised firebrick and had a very complicated shape inside. The Wolf had been repairing one of the furnaces (a wonderful job he made of it) and I got one of the reject firebricks. I carved a recessed shape of a cross in it, surreptitiously heated the brick, and carefully poured in molten zinc, using a large ladle such as was used for clearing off dross. Very pleased to see it cool nicely, I then rubbed it smooth on concrete and polished it. It seemed to shine and was a nice thing to have in my pocket. It got confiscated in a search – hope some Nip enjoyed it.

We managed to get two coke stoves installed in the rest room. These smelled and blackened the room and I guess did the same to our minds. Result – snarling and snapping and moaning, due to deleterious fumes no doubt. Sergeant Lew Munn, East Surrey Regiment, in the next bed space to me, was in charge of the other shift and he and I realised that something had to be done. So we started up short lectures at the midday or midnight breaks.

Icy winds howling up the valley blew snow through broken window panes and through the vent slits overhead, and the black-out curtains were blown about.

For myself, I began to hate that rest room and preferred to stand over an unused simmering furnace. Many an hour I spent with Casey Hoyle talking over one of these, and it was by furnace No. 4, in February 1945, that we had a mutual experience of realisation of "Truth". This was to affect us both deeply and pleasantly through the next months – up to release in fact.

I had acquired a bible somehow – it cost me quite a few cigarettes. I split it into Old and New Testaments and bound them, using Denkai filter cloth and an old Nip shirt, and glued them with the molasses mixture used for "tacking up" the driving belts in the factory. This was so I could put one of them in my pocket and use it when and if. It was from the book of Proverbs that Casey and I did some very helpful meditations walking along the path over the river.

Casey Hoyle

Casey was a Company Sergeant Major in the Manchester Regiment. He had been a champion boxer. Fairly short but stocky, cleft chin and square face. A remarkable character. I was certainly fortunate in meeting up with him.

It had been my practice to kneel and say prayers. In the rather close quarters of prison this was probably provocative. I once had things thrown at me. My next door PoW, Lew Munn, used to complain that I was being holier etc. But it got round to Casey that I was a Christian and one day he asked me to give an account of my belief. This involved going through my life. So we agreed that I would give as fully as possible the whole of it and he would listen without comment. I asked him to do the same. We had plenty of time. So in the course of many journeys to and fro, I was paid the considerable compliment of hearing about life in a Lancashire working class home. Very unusual, as might be expected. He loved T.E. Lawrence, Palestine, Egypt and the Arabs. In the course of the next six months of intimate friendship, he told me from his own personal experiences more about the Middle East than I could have learned elsewhere. Jerusalem, Cairo and Petra, which he loved. I felt I had almost been there. But that was in his tour of service. He also told of life in Manchester as a boy. There was that wonderful old friend, a schoolmaster, who had befriended him. Such small details as the reprimand he got for cleaning up the old chap's bicycle, "That's mud from Herefordshire! I want it left there!" From the same source Casey got his deep love and knowledge of the books of George Borrow.

My Life

It was not Casey who taunted me with having led a sheltered life. It was my neighbour in the barrack room. Having been in the meat trade in London, he had some pretty startling stories to tell – he had not lived at all a sheltered life! But Casey, on the other hand, listened in the way I think he must have listened to his old school-master, with real interest. Rather a new experience for me to have such an audience. Also a challenge to be honest and not hide or avoid anything on my part.

So I went through my life and beliefs.

The Billets (Funatsu)

There was a period of some weeks when hardly any of us spoke. There was just no energy left. There were several feet of snow out-side and a howling wind. The walls of the building were double wood only and the small windows were single panes of glass. Three small charcoal fires to heat a long room housing eighty or ninety men. A bit of a scramble to get a place round the stove, and the inevitable shoving and pushing. We had soon realised that the five blankets had only kapok filling, and were about as much good as two decent woollen blankets. Thank heavens for British Army great-coats. We slept in every stitch of clothing we possessed.

On a pint of cooked rice and a thin "daigon" stew we had to battle our way in darkness to the factory along a narrow groove in the snow – mountainside to the right, steep slope to the river on the left.

Christmas – a Bright Light in the Darkness

We did not see much in return for the efforts at home with regard to Red Cross. But it may be some consolation that we did each receive one whole food parcel from American Red Cross at Christmas, and the one-and-a-half boxes that we received over the next two months quite literally saved our lives. The benefit was mental as much as physical.

What vows we vowed over coffee creams! And raisins – stupendous! As for the bar of chocolate, I made one cube (my self-imposed daily allowance) last all the way from camp to factory on Boxing Day night.

Lew Munn's shift was also on nights, and on Christmas Eve, and by dint of much talk, he arranged that if we "worked hard" the Denkai (plate room) could start their second strike early. We in the Denkillo (furnaces) were allowed to finish when the Denkai was ready. This was at 2 a.m. on Christmas morning. Before we went back to camp I led them singing a few carols to help that Christmas feeling a bit, and also, in spite of consequences, to show the Nips that even under these conditions we still had a bit of song left in us.

But now! Imagine how thrilling it was, just as we were singing *Land of Hope and Glory*, the air raid siren went. This was one of the first and was a real excitement. It was a sort of timely greeting from friends.

Then it was over the snow by bright moonlight back to camp, for four hours sleep and to wake up on Christmas Day with a free day in front of us. Oh, those Red Cross boxes! What nectar for mouth and mind. A concert and my carol party helped to make a surprisingly good Christmas for us. That day we did not seem to notice the cold so much. In fact, I wandered outside in the evening to watch for a few moments a most wonderful, crystal clear, frosty starlight night, and to "tune in" particularly carefully to home for a few minutes, and blow the cold.

For a while I had forgotten the blank hopelessness that sometimes came over me. Much later, after release, in the 5th Replacement Camp in Manila, I had an attack of desolation, though the physical situation was lovely round the camp – trees and a stream, and some rather welcome solitude; but I offered to God a hearty prayer of thanks – the actual fact of freedom struck right home.

Poetry

I had Palgrave's *Golden Treasury* with me most of the time. What a boon it was! And Marie Corelli's novel, *Ardath*, influenced and encouraged me much. My "journey" was helped by that of Tobias and his angel.

By now it was springtime. May/June in Japan is lovely and the hillside opposite camp was covered in azaleas. Time to clean the window behind my bed-space. Felt it was time to do the same within self too. Thomas Carlyle's poem really gave one a bit of hope for the day – a sort of morning prayer:

> So here hath been dawning
> Another blue day:
> Think, wilt thou let it
> Slip useless away?

> Behold it aforetime
> No eye ever did.
> So soon it for ever
> From all eyes is hid.

Employed in Cemetery and in Camp – Change

For various reasons I asked to be removed from the factory. Orrocks was decent enough to put me on the newly started, so-called "gardening" party. We started out a little after the denkai men and then had a very pleasant walk of seven kilometres through villages and past temples and terraced paddy fields. A total of fourteen km a day, added to the hours digging in this old cemetery, hoeing, fish-manuring and bonfire making, was a bit tiring given our diet. But it was spring time. May/June in Japan is the best anywhere.

A charming sight on the walk to the cemetery. In the doorway of a typical wooden house in one village, two little girls crooning happily, making the sweetest sounds. Another scene. Approaching a small wayside temple we see a young woman all done up with baggy trousers and top-knot with her baby on her back. She stops, faces temple, bows, claps her hands several times, waits, bows and then walks on.

The path over the steep bank narrows because a large boulder has crashed down from the hills above. Just there is a little shrine with small statues, one headless, and flower pots with a few flowers. I imagine that someone was killed there.

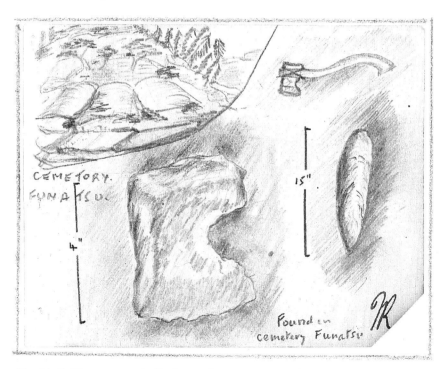

Fig. 21. PoWs set to work digging up Jap cemetery to plant sweet potatoes. Very ancient places – deep black earth – many interesting finds from Neolithic times. Japs did not like my construction of axe. Lovely chestnut trees. Funatsu, Japan, 1944/45.

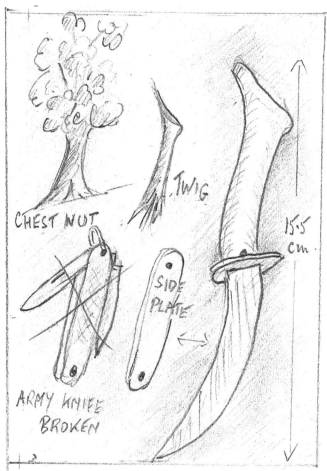

Fig. 22. Chestnut tree in Jap cemetery where we were set to planting sweet potatoes, 1944. Smashed army knife – side plate worn down on concrete and bashed into shape. This knife still in constant use, 2000 AD (see picture to left)

A farm house by the cemetery – quite small and rural. There we sat to have our Yasumi break. Out came a young woman with a child and sat and talked with us. We said that the guard would probably shout. She made as if to say "pouff" to him. Next day or so I brought her the very last squeeze from a tube of Nivea cream. She took it, went into the house and came back with some chrysanthemums for us. The talk was, as usual, about babies and children, with terrific interest in any photos we still had.

Recurring bouts of fever had undermined me, like most, and I had to drop out of the garden detail.

The Loaf and the Prayer, or the Prayer Loaf

Back in camp several men were pretty ill. An American had got himself unpopular for stealing. He had got beriberi badly. Beriberi begins with the feet, rises up until it gets to the heart, and can kill. The MO managed to keep him alive. But I thought I should do something and visited him regularly in sick bay. Got him to talk in detail about his home life. Ian Wethey had done the same for me in the jungle.

But in praying for him I got it into my head that I should do something in the way of an offering as well. Lunch ration for the "cemetery party" included a rather nice little loaf of bread. Could I show my sincerity by offering up half – floating it down a little stream? I did.

In fact this chap, whose name was Elmer J. Blazus, survived, and was one of the first to be taken off from camp early. His wife wrote to me some months later and thanked me for keeping Elmer going just long enough.

Boiler Man

I was once again indebted to Lieutenant Orrocks, our camp officer, who appointed me as boiler man in the cookhouse. There I was in charge of the vertical steam boiler. After a bit of instruction from a Scottish engineer PoW, I got the hang of injecting cold water into the pressurised boiling water in the top section of the contraption. I had to take the two taps and juggle them so that the venturi tube on the steam line, which narrows and increases pressure, could "pick up" the cold water in the other line and inject it into the boiler. Much watching of the glass gauge. I really enjoyed this job. "My" steam did the cooking, and also heated the water in the communal bath via a pipe. We could use the bath after the Nips.

We had a prayer meeting round the back, by the boiler. Interrupted by a Nip guard, I said "Kami no Uta" (God songs): "A so deska" – and with some haste he removed himself. You have to be careful how you go where gods or ancestors are concerned. That is what seems to be the main thrust of Shinto. All right as far as it goes, but it doesn't say much about the treatment or care for fellow humans outside the family or Nippon. Poor Private Mann, who had tried to escape in a fit of madness, was finally beaten to death by Furishima. (Furishima later swung for it after War Crimes trials.)

Hope in the Air

They started giving us things! That was mid-August. It was a great day when we watched working parties return to camp, one by one, shortly after leaving. Of course, nobody knew anything, not even the Nips. This was just as well, for if local inhabitants or soldiery had been informed of the state of things in Tokyo, we should have probably been molested, or worse.

I was lucky in that I still had my job to do with the boiler. Rumours flying. Remarkable calmness in camp. Men idle of course, but too emaciated to create trouble. Someone went to demand axes from Nip sergeant. When Orrocks took men to the police station to search for arms they found the firing pins of the rifles had been filed off. Orrocks quite bravely went off by rail to find out what was happening.

Into the camp on 1st September, and not until then, came some Swedish Red Cross people. Their object was to inspect and report – not actually very interesting to us.

The real excitement came when on 4th September some US Air Force fighter planes swooped up the valley and dipped wings to us. Then came the B29s. They circled round high up and then let out coloured parachutes all over the hillside. Quite a lot smashed. Parties went up the hillside into the trees and recovered the containers. Clothing and food. Chocolates and cigarettes. I got myself a decent wind jacket. We had to send some of the goodies up to the hill-camp by cable railway.

Colonel Johnson, US Army/Air Force, 5th September

This handsome air ace, bristling with weapons and decorations, was to us a wizard or an angel. He stood on a table and let us know that we were rescued. Did we cheer him! He told us to behave like soldiers. We were now under military discipline. This last came just in time, for the Yanks among us (what a crowd they were) were getting mutinous. He promised that we should be out and away from Japan just as soon as he could fix it. He had to get over to other camps. Several US troops were with Johnson – great tall well-fed men, all looking embarrassed; they had got the idea that we would be barmy.

Some Journey

True to his word, within three days the trains were commandeered at pistol point and we were on our way. Breakfast finished, we were "fell in" and marched out of the camp gates, Union Jack leading. Just left everything, cookhouse, boiler and all. Marched (walked) down the track and through the village; saw some bemused villagers to whom we threw cigarettes, and once again onto the narrow-gauge bogeys. At the junction with the main line there was a crowd which seemed to include Nips. I think it was at this point that some of our officers were relieved of the samurai swords they had so recently acquired.

The mainline train came, and once again there was this business of being separated. Casey Hoyle went one way, waved, and I was on my own again. We were whizzed down to the coast, where we got out and on to landing craft manned by lanky US marines. We were taken out to a hospital ship – the USS *Rescue*. Stripped and checked for disease, lice, etc.

Woke up in a nice bunk. Eyes open to find a lovely, white nurse, who gave me some chocolate. Got some advice about not gorging myself. Actually the ship's bakery had the machinery set to maximum light for the bread. Slept a lot.

Yokohama, 9th September 1945

Woke up in Yokohama. Quayside full of all sorts of stores, equipment, etc. I sorted out some US uniform shirts and trousers and handed the heavy woollen British Navy kit to a sailor. Saw Fujiyama in the distance. Also saw squads of other PoWs passing. They had various uniforms on, including kit looted from Nips. Ate too much. Saw Nips scavenging bread and pork! Wrote letters home. Found this note book. Last entry: "Thank God I am one of the 50% who survived three and a half years of captivity under semi-civilized people."

Repatriation

That is the last entry in the 'Service Writing Tablet' that I came by on the quayside in Yokohama. I filled 87 pages in pencil during the sea trip from Manila to San Francisco on the *Marine Shark*, 9th October to 1st November 1945. Also during this voyage I did two dozen or so pencil sketches.

I also kept a proper diary in a small black notebook, covering the last days in prison to my arrival in Southampton, 20th August to Sunday 18th November. After three and a half years of captivity in Malaya, Siam and Japan, my diary entry for 7th September 1945 reads: *Breakfast finished – walk out of cookhouse – leave everything including boiler burning. Fall in – right turn – out of prison camp with Union Jack leading.*

A month later, Monday 8th October: *US Army Replacement Camp, Manila: Join the 'racketeers' – draw two beers, three oranges, coffee, bread and jam. Meet Filipino boy – bargain for bananas in exchange for cigars. Banana boy does not come back – gave cigars to Jap PoWs. Get ticket No. 1027 HAH. Nice supper, walk, bed.*

Fig. 23. So-called "Fifth Replacement Camp", Manilla. Many U.S. personnel there with ex-prisoners very well and respectfully treated: superb rations; open-air cinema. We were here for some weeks (14th September to 9th October 1945).

Tuesday 9th: *Rise early – today we go home – lovely thought. Hope we're not mucked about – don't know whether Canada or USA. Clean up after tiffin – acquire decent mess kit. Called out and leave camp 5-ish, on board 6-ish – USS Troopship "Marine Shark".*

Wednesday 10th: *7.30 a.m. out of harbour – breakfast. Start writing up PoW story – find good place to be alone – up steps behind bridge structure.*

Friday 12th: *Out into beautiful smooth Pacific – me perched in cubby hole, file nails. Sail into sunrise. A good Friday.*

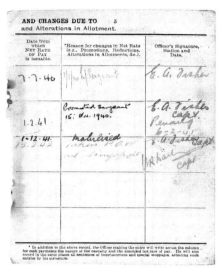

Leaf from my
Service Pay Book
Removed rest of book
because had to carry
everything.

Fig. 24. Leaf from John's paybook.

Fig. 25. Prisoner of War Medal, carrying on the reverse the inscription
"Intrepid against all adversity".

Malayan Government Accounts Office,
Hope House,
45, Great Peter Street,
London, S.W.1.

Please quote my ref 2/Nom/1515
in all correspondence.

Date 13. XII. 45

Sir,

I have the honour to inform you that your Volunteer account has now been written up to the end of your leave. This account, which has been prepared by the Army Pay Corps, has been credited with any balance of pay due at the date of capitulation and, with effect from that date, with pay etc. at regular forces rates including normal increments, war service increments, Japanese campaign pay, ration allowance and war service gratuity.

The balance of your account after deducting advances amounts to £

Under instructions from the Colonial Office a reserve of 10% on the gross credits to the account with a minimum of £50 is to be retained for the time being to meet contingencies. This reserve will be dealt with later when I have received and posted all advance accounts and instructions are received from the Colonial Office with regard to its disposal

630 : 10: 6

£67: 0: 0.

Leaving a balance now payable amounting to

£563:10: 6

I have requested the Crown Agents for the Colonies to remit you the balance now payable. Owing to shortage of typing assistance it is not possible to enclose a copy of your account. A copy will, however, be prepared and sent to you as soon as possible. In the meantime it is requested that you will be good enough to refrain from making enquiries with regard to rates of pay, allotment allowances to dependants etc. as particulars will be shown in your account.

I have the honour to be,
Sir,
Your obedient Servant,

Malayan Government Accountant.

To: J. H. READ Esq
20 Court Road
Tunbridge Wells

V.2.

Fig. 26. Letter summarising arrears of pay.

75

John Hanson Read
Ordained Priest
in Chichester Cathedral
on F. of S. Thomas 1951
by me
George Crest

CATHEDRAL

ST MARY EASTBOURNE

ST WILFRID BRIGHTON

ST MARY BEDDINGTON

ST MARK HORSHAM

St MARY T St PETER . PETT

St LAURENCE . GUESTLING

Fig. 27. Significant churches.

3
And after

Back in UK

On Sunday 18th November 1945 I arrived in Southampton on the Queen Mary having left Japan on 9th September. Did my last Kitchen Personnel duty in the ship's kitchens and diner. Went up onto lifeboat deck and spotted Elizabeth and Christopher on the quayside. Amazing. But had to wait a long time. Men of the well-known regiments were called first. Straits Settlements Volunteer Force very much the last call. Elizabeth and Chris had spotted me. After a rather brief greeting I had to get on a lorry to be taken to rehabilitation centre. Clever them managed to find out where it was and somehow got there. Lovely walk: chiefly memorable for the kicking up of the dry beech leaves. Elizabeth had to go off. Chris and I found beer and fish and chips, which were for me absolute bliss. Chris had to go off. I attended clothing centre to be issued with my de-mob clothing allowance. This included a brown pin-striped double-breasted suit. A few months later I was to wear this same brown suit to a wedding in Exeter Cathedral – and not one raised eyebrow from my godmother's family and friends in their pre-war wedding finery.

Arriving (how, I can't remember) at home in Court Road, Tunbridge Wells, found Mother and Father and Susan there. Wherever was one to begin! They had all been through the traumas of wartime Britain; I had rather unrealistic anticipations from freedom. So it was not all that easy for any of us.

Back to Work

There was to be three months repatriation leave. No such thing as debriefing in those days.

The only ex-PoW I met was "Porky" Gardner from Penang days in the Mercantile Bank of India. He was living in Sussex. I put my name down at the employment exchange for organ building. There was no response. But later I was approached by the Head Office of M.B.I. and in due course went back to the city. I had lodgings in Ealing. One of my jobs in the bank was to calculate the gratuities payable to staff (including me) in respect of "Suffering endured in the bank's service". It varied according to seniority. Mine was about £5000 – which helped pay for university fees at Oxford later.

In head office things seemed to be little changed. I don't recall hearing of any of the many others of the Far-Eastern staff having been prisoners or if they went back to the east. However, one day I was feeling in need of refreshment during the morning and was about to leave the bank to go over to the Grapes pub in Leadenhall Market. But a loud voice called out "Where do you think you are going?" This was one of the Messengers on duty at the swing door. "You are not in the East now, Sah!" I think the process of change began there!

Next there was a conversation with one Wintersgill about choirs and church in general. He remarked with some feeling that if he had the chance he would offer himself for the ministry of the C of E. That set me thinking.

Next bit of the process was hearing a sermon from the Vicar of Rusthall Church, Tunbridge Wells. What were we going to give to God in thankfulness for safety and freedom? Was it to be cash or service or ourselves? The point went home. I spoke to him at the church door. Things moved at breakneck speed from that moment. I was called to be interviewed in Church House, Westminster. A phone message from there to St John's College, Oxford. If I could be in college in a few days there was an ex-service place for me as an undergraduate. That was a third surprise. Yes, I had got Matric exemption through School Certificate (mostly languages) all those years before.

The next thing to do was to clear it with the bank. I got an appointment with Mr Crichton, the General Manager. When I told him of the situation he just stood up with a smile and congratulated me, saying that if the church was served as well as the bank had been by me, they were going to get a good man. He then told me that he was an elder in the Presbyterian Church.

Whatever Next: Religious Conditioning

One had got used to extraordinary things happening over the years. Quite undeserved blessings. There was this warm feeling that things were going to unfold for me. I prayed of course, and wondered. If there was an openness to Providence, it came out of quite long years of religious practice and experience. Sunday school in Bournemouth, going with Father to church, over five years as a chorister in the Abbey with psalms, scripture, sermons, hymns and anthems all surrounding me from the age of nine. Then confirmation in Henry VII chapel and regular communion. From the Choir School I went, as did many ex Choristers, to Hurstpierpoint College, a Woodard school and specifically Christian. In London I had been living with a devout churchgoing family. Then, in Malaya, I joined the Church choirs in Penang and Kuala Lumpur. In captivity it was obvious that one resorted to prayer often. Bible study and discussion with fellow PoWs helped us all. Enforced asceticism brought meditation and the beginnings of contemplation readily and effectively into practice.

So it was not very surprising that, in Rusthall church, an old clergyman's challenge to give oneself to God had fallen on ready ears. I am often asked if there were any blinding flashes of illumination, or if it was my experience in prison that propelled me into the ministry as a clergyman. Well, yes to both. But there are degrees of inspiration, and the ones given to me arose from many places and people. Like many Christians I, and they, feel truly that, as the gospel of St John, Chapter 15 verse 16, puts it *Ye have not chosen me, but I have chosen you.* There really is no question of being somehow deserving or being better than anyone else.

Oxford

Father and I drove to Oxford in our old Austin car. He deposited me at the main gate of St John's College. Not that the big gate was opened for me. The little postern gate was open. A visit to the porters' lodge showed me where to go. And thus I found myself in a pleasant couple of rooms up staircase No. 6 in North Quad.

I had no idea what I was letting myself in for, but a call to visit Professor Geoffrey Lampe introduced me to the two other undergraduates who were also going to read Theology. They were Peter Snow and Glen Jenkins. Peter was of Anglo Catholic persuasion and seemed to be well informed about things. Glen on the other hand was about as bewildered as I was. Dear old Glen had recently been in the RAF. In Hall for supper for the first time, when meal was finished he picked up his knife, fork and spoon. Sheer habit from service days. Highly embarrassed in front of laconic young undergraduates. He used often to recall this in fun. We were all three ex-service men for whom places had been reserved by the college.

In those days every undergraduate had what was known as a moral tutor as well as a study tutor. Mine was one Professor Colin Roberts, a famous papyrologist. He informed me that I would have to master New Testament Greek. I had none at all. He promised to help me if I would put in an hour's study before breakfast every day. I would also be required to know the texts of important early church documents in Greek.

I had to knock on Colin's door and then wait for a few minutes while he carefully closed down the sheets of glass on his desk which held in place scraps of papyrus recovered from the sands of the island of Elephantine in the Nile river. It was Colin who identified one slip with a fragment of St John's gospel in Greek from the early second century AD. This major discovery caused scholars to revise the dating of the gospel.

Glen, Peter and I were very fortunate in having Geoffrey Lampe as our tutor. He was to become Regius Professor of Divinity in Cambridge. One could not have had a wiser or kinder person to guide us through what were for us uncharted lands. Geoffrey took me home to meet his wife Elizabeth. I would baby-sit for them. Later came a memorable holiday when they took me to the Edinburgh Festival.

Fellow theologians with us at St John's were Hugh Montefiore and Kenneth Woolcombe. Both were to get firsts and to become Bishops. Geoffrey Lampe and others must have worked quite hard on the authorities to maintain confidence in us three. We inevitably ended up with third class honours. Thanks are certainly due to the college for seeing us through. Actually it could be noted that we must have been endued with colossal optimism and perseverance.

I was certainly very appreciative of the privilege and dignity of it all. Lectures by top-ranking theologians in the halls of other colleges. Hours spent in libraries. All the distractions of social and sporting activities to say nothing of gorgeous girls, and chaps, who gave the impression of owning the place. We three were ten years older than most people.

There were of course regular services in chapel. We would also go to other churches, high and low, as well as the university Church, St Mary's. I was involved in the Student Christian Movement and took part in a University Mission.

My main occupation outside study was with the St John's Madrigal Society, which one Conrad Brann and I started. I like to think that we (there were thirteen of us) were quite good. We did Madrigal tours in Germany and in Denmark. This last was splendidly arranged by Hans Lorentzen, a Danish pastor.

A few of us responded to a challenge from Mrs Lane Poole, the President's wife. It was to give up some time in the vac to go and help in a holiday camp in Maldon. This was for severely deprived youngsters from the East End. We were required to read their case histories. Needless to say we had plenty to open our eyes!

Birmingham

The next step for us theologians was to theological college. I was lucky enough to get to Queens College, Birmingham. I remember arriving in a bit of a state. A fear I had was that I would be faced with a lot of dark and dismal men, all terribly holy and demanding that everything had to be given up and time must be spent in endless services and self denial. Nightmare indeed!

The old part of the college had been the residence of Bishop Gore. It was not a very lovely place. Austere and Victorian. On the other hand the Chapel was a fine building made to the design of Canon Cobham, the excellent principal. It was brick-built to a Byzantine design with a lovely apsidal east end. The text over the door reminded us ". . . you did not choose me, but I chose you". Jock, as we called Canon Cobham, was a great inspiration. His quiet manner and evident spirituality made him a valuable role model for aspiring clergy. He and his sister were keen on alpine flowers and would be off to Switzerland every year.

The General Ordination Exam (G.O.E.) was what we worked for. Lectures would include biblical subjects, devotion, pastoralia, and, of course homiletics (sermon preparation and delivery).

Off-duty activities included squash and tennis. Light-hearted efforts produced entertainments in the form of sketches etc. There was quite a lot of talent amongst students, and some good musicians.

Jock had travelled a lot on the continent. He brought over several students from Germany, Switzerland and Denmark. There was Hans Brink Jensen and his lovely wife Elsie. Also Hans Christian Lorentzen. With both of these I made lasting friendships to be continued by Frances and our children. Jock also introduced us to music and liturgies from Maria Laach. This was at the start of the Parish Communion movement. We had visits too from priests of the Eastern Orthodox church.

All in all, Queens gave us wonderful insights into the life of the wider church.

Eastbourne and Ordination

I was lucky enough to arrive at the necessary sponsorship from the Parish of St Mary, Eastbourne, and Canon Lewis Meredith, the Vicar. It was there I duly went to prepare for ordination.

So I was ordained deacon in Chichester Cathedral by Bishop George Bell at St Thomastide 21st December 1950. Not the best time for dear family and people from St Mary's Eastbourne to travel across Sussex to Chichester. It was a memorable service with my old music master, H.A. Hawkins (Hawkey), at the organ. I wouldn't say I was a favourite of his but I was certainly one of Hawkey's boys, what with music and trumpet etc. at Hurst. And so after 12 years and a whole wartime history, it was amazing to have Hawkey plus his trumpeters from the Royal Sussex Regiment for my ordination.

Back in Eastbourne I first stayed with the Merediths in the Vicarage. After a bit they found me lodgings in Bay Pond Road, right by the churchyard. And so my life began as a clergyman, and what is known as the "serving of my title". This involved visiting, youth work, services, preaching and study of set books for priests' exams after a year. This exam was held in Diocesan Church House in Hove. Top floor with glass roof, blazing sun, and a man with a scratchy pen, to say nothing of my headache (malaria), produced poor results. At the ordination service the rather sour archdeacon presenting me to the bishop for priesting said "I have examined (me) and you (bishop) are going to ordain him". He did.

Frances and Marriage

I look back with warm thankfulness to the hospitality of Lewis and Evelyn Meredith at the Vicarage. And it was there, at a Canasta party, that I first met Frances Parkin, hot from London University. Against all probability she allowed me to ask her out. And later amazingly answered my proposal of marriage with only a very slightly delayed yes.

We were married in St Mary's by Lewis Meredith on 24th May 1952. In those happier days this was known as Empire Day. Both Frances' parents and her family were there. My family too with the exception of my father, who was too frail. Bridesmaids Eileen Hartley and Susie McGilp and my best man Peter Stirk. It was a lovely day, a full church and St Mary's bells, a generous present from the ringers. A handsome reception at the Cumberland

Fig. 28. Engaged.

Hotel on Eastbourne sea front. Then Frances and I were sent off in a hired Austin car towards Midhurst. We had a picnic tea, packed by the thoughtful hotel staff. This was at Wilmington, looking over the Cuckmere valley towards Firle Beacon. Ever since this has been a favourite picnic place for us.

Our honeymoon at the Luttrell Arms in Dunster brought us almost under the wall of the castle where lived some distant relatives of mine, the Luttrells. We visited the castle but, to my mother's displeasure, not as anything more than tourists! We took in

Fig. 29. Married.

Dunkery Beacon and a cream tea, where also we found a lovely illustrated copy of Omar Khayyam. Glastonbury and Minehead; Grabbist Hill near Dunster where Mrs Alexander (1880) wrote *All things bright and beautiful* and *the purple headed mountain*. Through thick fog to Barnstaple and its bridge and thoughts of Frances' father. At Bridgewater we found a notice "No Bore today!" Then to Athelney where in 1698 a workman had unearthed the Alfred Jewel. Then back *via* Oxford to see Father and Aunt Dorothy and so home.

Setting Up Home – Eastbourne

A kind parishioner had obligingly gone abroad and lent us her bungalow. We were to look after her cat! Dear Mrs Dyer! The first of many generous parishioners who over the years were to help us on our way. She was to leave her bungalow to the church as residence for the curate.

There followed some truly happy years in and around St Mary's Church in Old Town, Eastbourne. We next went to live in a chauffeur's cottage in Pashley Road, rebuilt after a direct hit in a Hit and Run raid. The Parkin family had been living further up the road at No. 10 – too close for comfort. In April 1953 our son Anthony was born. Photos taken at this time and in subsequent years remind us of the joy he brought to us all.

Horsham

Life in the parish went on happily enough largely thanks to our vicar Lewis Meredith and his wife Evelyn. But after four happy years it was time to move. We responded to an advertisement in the Church Times. I went to be curate-in-charge of St Mark's Church, Horsham, under the Rev'd Ronnie Goodchild, later Bishop of Kensington. It was a great benefit to be in a team of clergy in Horsham.

In 1955 our daughter Judith was born at home in Wellington Road adding to our family happiness.

There we made many good friends including our doctor, John Dew. Laurence and Marion Culshaw lived in Lambsbottom, a lovely old house backing on to the Park. Sidney and Margaret Martin made us ever welcome in Kings Road and were always a real blessing. We are still in touch with both families.

At St Mark's Church we had good congregations, especially at morning services. It was there that we were initiated into the mysteries of Old Tyme Dancing at the excellent parish parties.

Brighton

When a letter came from Bishop Bell asking us to consider moving to St Wilfrid's Brighton, it seemed right to agree. The Bishop wanted me to introduce Parish Communion, with communicants. Hitherto, St Wilfrid's had followed the full Anglo-Catholic pattern of the so-called Wagner parishes of Brighton, Wagner being the name of a wealthy Victorian priest who had remarkably been able to impose his ways upon five of the Brighton parishes. In these parishes there would have been one or more early services with communicants and then a full High Mass with few if any communicants.

This was rather like throwing me to the lions. With the exception of Hutch, Canon Charles Hutchinson of St Bartholomew's, these other priests managed to be dismissive of the Bishop, and of me too.

We did, however, have a very nice Vicarage, the old Garton House in fact, hitherto a Mother and Baby home! But best of all, our darling Jonny was born there. He would not wait for the doctor. The midwife was with us and helped Frances in a smooth and beautiful delivery. I was there and very proud of her. Our upstairs lodger, "Big" Judith, came down to wish Frances well and was told to go and look into the Moses basket. She was completely unaware of what had been happening underneath her flat during the night. Dear old Hutch came and gave Jonny such a blessing he hardly needed baptising!

In our four years at St Wilfrid's we were able to enjoy what Brighton had to offer. There were the Downs and the beaches, Stanmer Park with picnics and kite flying. There were our visits to Parkin grandparents in Eastbourne. Then holidays with Mardi (Frances' sister) and Derek and the three big cousins in Dover – the highlight of each year.

Tony started school at Ashdown House. He had been diagnosed with knock knees at Horsham and now had to endure being in leg irons. He very bravely put up with this, specially at school. But came a day when a locum consultant saw him. He asked Tony if his home had an upstairs. He was told to go right up and throw the leg irons out of the window!

Perhaps the best thing that happened to us in Brighton was the coming of Freia from Germany to be our *au pair*. If we had her with us for only nine months then, she is still one of the best loved friends we have. On her return to Germany she attended Heidelberg University, gaining high marks in English (of course). She married her Manfred. We visited her in Munstereifel and there have been several visits here with their family, Christa, Elke and Annette.

I can't say that I was very happy at St Wilfrid's what with the clear disapproval of the Anglo-Catholic clergy and one of the wardens. Bishop Bell had appointed me specifically to start "communion with communicants", in other words the Parish Communion. It was then 1957. There were two side altars as well as the high altar. There were six candlesticks on each one. I removed four such from the north side chapel, which had Hans Feibusch's murals (which we loved). There were of course complaints to the Bishop. However, this gave me a memorable phone conversation with Bishop Bell. He quite understood, but said that perhaps it should be done with consultation. He talked with me for twenty minutes – quite a privilege!

In those days Christian Aid was fairly new. One Janet Lacey had written a play designed to promote it in the parishes. She had made provision for some dance parts. We got some dancers from a local school of dancing. St Wilfrid's, with its lovely parquet flooring and moveable chairs, was a very suitable setting. A memorable presentation was not all that appreciated in the parish, but support came from the whole Deanery.

Our organist, Mr Pollard, was a loyal and friendly man. He gave Tony his first piano lessons

I was appointed part-time chaplain at Brighton General Hospital. In preparing for one ward service I had handed out hymn books. One therefore fell into the hands of a Roman Catholic lady. Next day I had a fairly angry visitor in the form of an RC priest complaining that I should have presumed to do such a thing.

In all this I must say that I always had approval from dear Canon Hutchinson. He had me down at St Bartholomew's to give a song recital. He also invited me to preach. It was after that Mass that one of the sisters attached to St Bart's made the comment to me saying "you are really quite nice", i.e. in spite of what the others are saying!

Beddington

In 1961 I had a letter from a Mrs Dorothy Bridges of Eastbourne. As she had been a parishioner of ours at St Mary's Church in Old Town she had been able to vet, as it were, both Frances and myself. This was rather relevant, as we now learnt that she herself was the patron of the benefice of St Mary's Beddington in Southwark Diocese. Her husband and his ancestors had been Rectors of St Mary's for long years. And so kind Mrs Bridges wrote asking us to consider taking up the living of St Mary's Parish.

With grateful hearts we took ourselves off to Beddington and found a lovely fourteenth century church and a fine Rectory. All of these within the setting of Beddington Park. The services at St Mary's were entirely acceptable, with early communion, followed by the 9.45 am Parish Communion. There was a well attended choral Evensong. The population of the parish was over 13,000. So there were plenty of baptisms and weddings. The offer was not to be refused. We moved to Beddington in August 1961.

We were to stay for 17 happy years. Our children went first of all to local Church schools. Tony, and then Jonathan, went on to Whitgift School in Haling Park, Croydon. Judy went to Sutton High School, a G.P.D.S.T. school. The family made very good use of the spacious rectory and garages. The large garden was quite productive. The park and lake were well used. The boys learnt to

Fig. 30. Impromptu family orchestra.

row there and earned holiday money helping with the boats. Judy's good hand-writing got her the job of writing up the marriage registers. There were often fifty weddings a year. Friendly and supportive parishioners made it a pleasure and a privilege for all of us.

Holidays

We often went to Farley Hill to stay with Susan. From her, as indeed from Elizabeth, we all had the happiest introduction to birds and beasts and country lore. Merry journeys to Dover to stay with Derek and Mardi. Never to be forgotten camping holidays in the New Forest and further afield. Happy visits to Earnley to join the Culshaws in picnics and swimming at West Wittering. And the local bus took me into Chichester for Evensong at the Cathedral.

A week on the Oxford Canal was a complete change, and great fun in spite of rain most days. Susan joined us and made sure we all took exercise on the tow-path. This holiday thanks to a legacy to Frances from a friend of her father's – they had served together in the R.A.S.C. in France in the Great War.

From Aunt Dorothy's legacy we got our Glenelg caravan. Never was a caravan more happily used. We were quite happy to do our caravanning in this country. Devon, Cornwall, the New Forest. The van came in useful too for lending and for the extra summer house that it provided. Also very good for revising for exams. A blessing indeed.

Parish Life

During all this time Frances ran our home and coped with most of the jolly business of feeding, clothing and schooling our three children. It has to be said that, though I worked from home, as the saying goes, too often the calls of duty took priority for me. Frances ran the Mothers' Union and Young Wives. She also taught part-time at Seton House, an independent kindergarten school in Carshalton. She then moved to the Link Special School in Bedding-ton as a class-room assistant – a very worthwhile experience. Her push-bike, dating from boarding-school in Bedford in the war, came into its own as transport to school.

I became Chairman of Sutton Moral Welfare Association, with its Mother and Baby Home in Sutton. I was Rural Dean of Sutton for five years 1965–1970. We began here our delightful association with 5th Beddington Guides and with Kath Chilcott and her family. With the Chilcotts and the Kimber family we also enjoyed fellowship with the Beddington ringers. We inherited a flourishing Youth Club – St Mary's Youth Fellowship (SMYF). In those days very few of them had cars or television. It did get more and more difficult as the years went by. But reunions of members years after were successful. I was a governor of Carew Manor Special School. This involved taking weekly assemblies with splendid singing of all sorts of choruses. Their carol services in Church were marvellous.

A new experience was becoming involved in the tradition of the May Queens. The annual service for all the groups in the South London area was always at St Mary's. Once or twice I took the wedding of a local girl whom I had crowned May Queen when she was a teenager.

Parish parties were great fun, and revealed hidden talents in young and old. As also at Harvest Supper entertainments. A complete surprise for me was a *This is Your Life* evening, complete with Red Book, to celebrate my 25th anniversary of ordination.

At a memorable visit to Bishop Stockwood for lunch at Bishop's House we met Dudley Tassell, Rector of St Mary, Rotherhithe. There ensued some very pleasant visits back and forth. They would bring a coach load of pensioners down for tea and Evensong at St Mary's. We would take up flowers for their Annual Fête. Strawberry teas would follow.

During our stay at Beddington we had several curates, Don Baker, John Sampford and Barry Compton. But rather specially we had Ian Thomas from Tasmania and his lovely wife Pat. They seized every opportunity for travel, study and fun while here. I got Ian to take my place preaching at the Tower of London. That was quite something for him.

There came a day when the Dean of Westminster wrote to me as Rural Dean of Sutton asking if any of the clergy in the Deanery would think of joining the ranks of visiting clergy at the Abbey. As an old chorister at the Abbey I jumped at the invitation. For the next thirty years I spent a week each year as Clergyman on Duty. The Dean's idea, started in 1966 for the nine hundred years' celebrations, and since emulated in many of our cathedrals, was to have, moving around in the Abbey, a priest who had no duties other than to be available to people. He had also to lead the two minutes prayer on the hour. The Dean provided a flat in the Little Cloister. The post was voluntary and though quite tiring being on foot most of the day, the sense of privilege in being part of the work of the Abbey was great. In meeting tourists and visitors from round the world, and in counselling many, there were some very interesting episodes. A professor from behind the Iron Curtain, permitted to visit the UK for a conference, unburdened himself: should he go back to his work and family, or should he defect? A few weeks later came a postcard from Hungary. He had made his difficult decision. Another day: two elderly ladies in great distress had travelled up from Mitcham. Would I please say a prayer for their dog, put to sleep that morning. No two days the same.

It was quite often the case that some big service, such as the Judges Service, meant that one had a ringside seat. The Visiting Clergy had their own stall for Evensong. Early services were in St Faith's chapel, where I had been prepared for confirmation in 1931.

Departure from Beddington

Altogether our time at Beddington was very happy and fulfilling. But my past history as a PoW under the Japs began to catch up with me. So, after several years of asking, the Bishop of Chichester offered me the living of the joint parishes of Guestling and Pett. There we came in the snow with a lovely welcome from Bishop Peter Ball, the newly appointed Bishop of Lewes. This was in 1978.

Guestling and Pett

At first I was appointed as only Priest in Charge of the two parishes, that is, one who is only licensed for a term according to the Bishop's will. At Beddington I had been Rector, with freehold, but now I had to resign that freehold. However, all was settled when the two parishes had been legally united into one benefice and I was duly instituted as Rector.

There followed five happy years of parish work. Pett Church is a Victorian building in the centre of the village. Guestling Church is a pretty building, fairly heavily restored after a fire in the last century. There is also St Nicholas's Chapel down near the beach. It used to be the shed for storing rocket apparatus for reaching ships wrecked in Rye Bay.

A Country Parson

It didn't take us long to realise the priorities of village life. The day we moved into the Rectory our Pett Churchwardens asked if I had fixed my summer holiday. I hadn't. We quickly learned that the last Saturday in July was the Pett Horticultural Show. Families would be back! The Rector must be there! The Summer Fête, held in the rectory garden, was the big day for the parish. In Guestling the Flower Festival was the highlight of the year. These events involved many who were not regular worshippers, but still felt a loyalty to their parish church. Typical of many C. of E. parishes I suspect.

In Beddington I had been a member of Wallington Rotary Club, and Speakers Secretary for some years. Now it was the Royal British Legion that I was invited (and expected) to join. Monthly meetings were held at *The Smuggler* at Pett Level. I took on the job of Welfare Officer and in time was elected a Vice President.

Remembrance Sunday meant full congregations. With so many names on the War Memorials of men with families still living in the villages, this was not surprising. The first year at Guestling my medals were checked over by a retired Wing Commander.

I had never lived in the country, in spite of moving around a lot while growing up. Initially some of the old farming families withheld judgement on this new Rector from the suburbs. When I was asked to join the select group guarding the marquee before the Pett flower show, I felt that I had been accepted. Wartime reminiscences were shared and friendships forged.

The Family

It seemed very quiet at the Rectory with all three children away from home.

Judy got her BA in English at Nottingham and her PGCE at Oxford Polytechnic. Tony got his BSc in Electrical Engineering at Kingston Polytechnic while working at Rediffusion Research. Jon was at Merrist Wood Agricultural College after a year as under-gardener at Westminster Abbey. They all came home at weekends to a joyful welcome from Titus, our Jack Russell, and they soon came to love the whole area.

Fig. 31. Christmas Day on Pett Level, 1978.

The churchwardens at Pett gave Jon the job of rebuilding part of the church wall. This he did during his summer vac. He used brickwork called Flemish Bond. We have a lovely photo of him at work taken by Tony. His delight in his work is obvious. This he certainly carried over into his landscaping later and his firm of *Border Landscapes* in and around Caterham.

Family group photos now showed six instead of five, when Judy got engaged to Simon Ellis. Simon's father was a friend from Malaya days, where we had enjoyed sailing, water-polo and golf together. As a civilian dentist, Peter had been interned in Changi. Amazingly we had met again on a street corner in Oxford when I was up at St John's. I was duly introduced to Peter's fiancée and was his Best Man at their wedding. In due course Peter became one of Tony's godfathers. Now our families were to be closely linked. Years later, Simon was to recall his father saying that I had told him "Now Peter, you must treat as many Japanese patients as you can".

Fig. 32. John and Frances.

Pett Level

Pett Level is a community in its own right, with many characters among its residents. A Saturday morning club based on St Nicholas' was good fun. I enjoyed it as much as the youngsters. The Pett Level Preservation Society had ensured that the area was safe from development. The Pett Level Rescue Boat was based behind *The Smuggler.* On Sea Sunday the crew brought the boat up to Pett Church.

We had visited the Pett Pools over the years in expeditions with my Aunt Mildred who had lived in St Leonards. She would have been thrilled by the flamingo that took up residence for our first summer in Pett. There was always something to watch. Binoculars were kept in the car. We gradually became more knowledgeable through joining the Pett Level Naturalists' Society. Monthly meetings were chaired by John Goodman. Each one different, each one fascinating – the only reason I left choir practice early!

Pilgrimages

Rye is the furthest deanery from our Cathedral. How many times have I been told that Canterbury, Rochester and possibly Southwark are all nearer than Chichester! The suggestion of a pilgrimage to Chichester by coach for St Richard's Day was greeted with enthusiasm. For some it was their first visit. As I was asked to organise a repeat of the day the next year, hopefully it was not their last.

Then one day a Pett parishioner, Arnold Ward, rang the door bell. Frances invited him in. "I shan't keep you long." He told us that his faith had been strengthened by a pilgrimage holiday to the Holy Land. "You two must go. Book it up with Inter Church Travel." A wonderfully generous man. He made just one condition: we must give a talk with slides on our return.

Along with several other latecomers, we joined a group led by the Rev'd Ralph Baldry from his Golders Green parish. We met at Heathrow. Any concerns we might have had about our leader were soon dispelled. Ralph was a man of great sensitivity and generosity. We extras soon felt welcomed into the group.

So many unforgettable scenes:

- a laden camel in among the morning rush-hour outside our hotel window;
- the beautiful Dominus Plevit Church – in the shape of a tear-drop – where Jesus wept over Jerusalem;
- the courtesy of the Coptic monk in the chapel on the roof of the Church of the Holy Sepulchre;
- the ancient olive trees in the Garden of Gethsemane;
- other visitors quietly joining our group in the ruins of the synagogue high up on Masada to hear Ralph reading from David Kossoff's account of the siege by the Roman army;
- the cloud coming down on us as we celebrated Communion on the roof of the church on the Mount of the Transfiguration;
- the mosaics in the chapel by the lake-side at Tabgha, where Jesus fed the 5,000;
- crossing the Sea of Galilee in a small open boat.

Everyone has their own special memories. And yes, looking towards Bethlehem from the Shepherds' Fields, and walking beside the Sea of Galilee, does give a new dimension to reading the Gospels.

Retirement

At the age of 66 I "proposed to take my retirement" as the archdeacon put it. This meant looking around for somewhere to live. This was not so easy, as the Pensions Board, to whom I applied for a loan, stipulated a low price for which there were few properties. We searched in Ninfield, Ringmer and Little Common. Eventually we fetched up across the valley in Icklesham. The acquisition of 6 Oast House Road was made possible only by the very generous assistance, once again, of my sisters Elizabeth and Susan, and a Pension Board mortgage.

Frances' sister Mardi was with us when the agent was taking us round. One property was too small and prim, but the agent had a new one on his list that day. We went straight round and, with Mardi's approval, decided that here was a possibility in spite of the dark brown paint everywhere. So we signed on. When Jon came down to see the place, he quickly saw the possibilities, especially the long kitchen with room for a dining area looking out on the garden. So we moved into No. 6 in July 1983.

Our Welcome to Icklesham

Almost before we were settled we had the warmest of welcomes from Edward and Olive Hayman. Edward's brother, Sam, had been our Rural Dean and Rector of Cheam, and a very good friend of ours. He had instructed them to visit us on our arrival in Pett. Now we were to enjoy their hospitality in Church Farmhouse on many occasions.

What Next?

An architect neighbour of ours, Maurice Wheeler, told me that I ought to be glad to be still needed, for, he said, there is no one more useless than a retired architect!

Well, over these last twenty years Frances and I have been kept going. She already had her commitment with Bishop Peter's Caring and Sharing scheme. She has continued as chair of the Deanery Support Committee for Diocesan Family Support Work.

Bishop Peter also installed me as Rural Dean of Rye. This involved pleasant visits round the parishes during the next 18 months. It was very different doing this job with no parish commitments. Two other retired clergy followed on after me. Rural Deans' meetings at Bishop Peter's home in Littlington always finished with warm doughnuts in the kitchen. Over the last 20 years or so, I think I have taken services in every parish in the Deanery to cover holidays and interregnums. Always a good welcome.

Relaxation

After large rectory gardens we missed growing our own fruit and vegetables, so soon took on a half-allotment in Winchelsea.

Fig. 33. Retirement (with beard).

Nothing like the first new potatoes and French beans! And nothing like the friendliness of fellow allotment holders, generously sharing excess seedlings along with words of wisdom. Flower Shows in Icklesham and Winchelsea became important dates in the diary.

There was time now for more music-making. I played flute in a small group, first in Icklesham and then at the home of Chris and Kate Davson in Mermaid Street, Rye. When Chris came down from his study telling us that we were "coming on", we really felt encouraged! There was also one pleasant arrangement when on

Thursdays I went first to Holy Communion in St Mary's and then to coffee with Elspeth Wrenn. I had the great privilege of having her accompany me singing right through Schubert's *Winterreise*, *Schwanengesang* and *Die schöne Müllerin*, etc., all 70 lieder.

I also joined the Winchelsea Singers. The annual Fun Evenings were hard work, but always surprisingly successful. The performances of sacred music in St Thomas's were a challenge, and the carol concerts an opportunity to sing something unusual as a solo – the *Appalachian Carol* one year and Stanford's *Monkey Carol* another. We were in good hands with our gifted conductor, Jean Taverner, with whom I also sang when she was organist at Icklesham.

Joining the Tuesday Painters Club of Rye opened up new opportunities. As children our mother had encouraged us all to sketch, and I had always taken paints on holiday. Now there was the challenge of portraits and still life, and, of course, having something ready for the Summer Exhibition. The Painting Weekends were highlights of the summer months, with welcoming hosts and a choice of gardens, farm buildings or local churches as subjects. The trips by coach up to Exhibitions in London were an added bonus and Frances often joined me on these expeditions.

Holidays

Holidays continued in our much-loved caravan. Our two favourite sites were visited at least once every year: East Ashling west of Chichester, so near for the Cathedral and the Festival Theatre and for visiting David Maundrell; and at Arlington, near Alfriston, within sight of the Downs. In both cases the site-owners became good friends, and we felt happily relaxed within five minutes of arrival.

Visits continued to my sister Susan, long since retired to Bonar Bridge in Scotland. Tony, Judy and Jon had all made the journey north, and they and their friends always found a great welcome. Four hours after leaving Euston you cross the border, and realise you're only half-way to Inverness! But we all love it up there.

We also visited Denmark. I had met Hans Christian Lorentzen and Hans Brink Jensen at Queen's, both pastors in the Danish Lutheran Church. Their families had visited us in Beddington. And so we stayed in Rønne on the island of Bornholm in the Baltic, and in Sønderho on the island of Fanø in the North Sea. Wonderful Copenhagen made a good half-way house. These were fascinating visits, giving us an inside view of Danish parish life and the opportunity to meet interesting people, who, of course, all spoke excellent English.

Happy Families

The 1980s saw the start of the enlargement of the family. Judy and Simon had been married at Guestling by Bishop Peter before we left. Tony married Kathi in beautiful Blumenstein church in the Bernese Oberland, and Jon married Roz in St Martin's, Epsom, another happy day. Tony had been working in Switzerland since

Fig. 34. Family group with grandchildren, 1996.

1980, and had sold his house in Epsom to Jon, whose firm *Border Landscapes* was soon to be based in Caterham. It has been a great joy to us that Tony is so much loved by his extended Swiss family and over the years they have all made us welcome.

And then came the grandchildren: David and Jonathan in Alton, Rebecca and Patrick in Hünibach, and Tim, Joanna and the twins Kate and Sophie in Caterham. We always looked forward to their visits, and with trips to the sea at Winchelsea Beach, and walks on the Firehills and in Guestling Wood, traditions were soon established.

Locum Duties

A new experience was doing locum duty abroad. In 1988 we went twice to St John's, Territet, on Lake Geneva, the Anglican church serving Montreux and district. One churchwarden was not impressed that I had been a mere clerk in my banking days in Malaya, and so had not socialised with the managers that he had known! Otherwise we had a very warm welcome and met interesting people in the regular congregation and among the English-speaking visitors.

We enjoyed living in St John's House, linked to the church, and Frances was thrilled to find the church library, tucked away behind the flower arrangers' cupboard, with books for sale as well as for borrowing. No garden, but who needed a garden with the peaceful Rose Garden beyond the church with the statue of the beautiful Empress Elizabeth of Austria? She had loved to visit Lake Geneva and tragically had been assassinated in 1898 as she boarded a lake steamer. And, of course, there was the walk beside the lake to Montreux, along the *Quai des Fleurs.*

We did warn the locum who was to follow me that main-line trains rushed past between the house and the lake, but he assured us this would be no problem as his boys were enthusiastic train-spotters. Happy memories, and we have kept in touch with St John's and returned for their mid-week service several times on later holidays.

Our first visit in April was well-timed, as we were able to visit Tony and Kathi in Berne and meet our granddaughter Rebecca. Also to hear Tony sing the part of Nanki Poo (at short notice) in the amazing production of *The Mikado* put on by St Ursula's, the Anglican church in Berne. That early training in the choir at Beddington must have stood him in good stead, and we were indeed proud parents. They played to packed houses for three nights and the British Ambassador was full of congratulations.

During our second visit in July, we entertained Bishop Ambrose Weekes. He was considering taking the post of Chaplain. "Show me round the parish, John." "There isn't a parish, Bishop." However, he made the decision to become Chaplain! We also had a jolly visit from Peter and Betty Harvey, *en route* for his regular summer chaplaincy on Lake Como. Tony and Kathi joined us for our last weekend and we proudly pushed Rebecca's pram along the *Quai des Fleurs* beside the Lake. A marvellous firework display for Swiss National Day, with a procession including William Tell and his young son, made a grand finale to our stay.

Fig. 35. John in Jon's garden.

Another year I did two weeks' duty at St Anne's, Alderney, formerly the garrison church, receiving typical island hospitality. They say that Alderney has only one import and one export: bottles. Perhaps it's just as well there is only one short stretch of road where drivers can exceed 30 mph. Here we saw a flock of yellow wagtails on migration, resting in the sand-dunes. What a treat!

A long interregnum in Icklesham, for the best part of six years, meant that I was kept pretty busy on Sundays, and taking weddings, baptisms and funerals. But not PCC meetings, as I was never officially in charge. It was a tonic once again to prepare adults for confirmation. We did sometimes remind each other "We are meant to be retired!" However, to be involved again with people in their times both of rejoicing and of sadness was a privilege, and made us feel really part of the village.

Visit to Dresden

The first to visit Freia and Manfred, soon after their marriage, had been Tony, just before his O-levels. No wonder he did well with his German oral! Now it was our turn. Our first visit was to Neunkirchen. Freia gave us a fascinating week. We visited Nürnberg, Coburg with the statue of Prince Albert in the market square, Bamberg – its cathedral now twinned with Chichester and, best of all, Rothenburg, where we walked round the walls of this historic town. The recording of organ music from St Jakob's church that we brought home brings back vivid memories of the church's 16th century carving of the Last Supper.

A good friend from my time as an ordinand at Queen's, Birmingham, John Beaumont, had visited Rothenburg in very different circumstances. No organ recital for him. John had jumped train while being transported from one PoW camp to another. He had holed up for a day down by the River Tauber, *en route*, as he hoped, to the Swiss frontier. Sadly this escape was no more successful than his other attempts, and John ended his years of captivity in Colditz.

Our second visit was to Dresden. After the fall of the Berlin Wall, Siemens had taken over failing factories in East Germany.

Manfred was sent to Dresden. His workers, queuing for breakfast half-an-hour before the canteen opened, were surprised when the new manager told them in local dialect that this wasted time would mean a deduction from their week's wages. As a schoolboy Manfred had escaped to West Germany with his mother – his memory served him well. Time-keeping and quality control were new concepts for these dispirited workers.

An American on his way back to the States had accosted us at Heathrow. He had seen Dresden on our luggage labels. "You must contribute to the re-building of the Frauenkirche." He went on his way. We needed no persuading. The devastation from that terrible air-raid was still there for all to see. But the church was rising again, a symbol for the future. At breakfast on our last morning, Manfred's newspaper had a front-page photo of the orb and cross which would be the gift of the British Dresden Society.

We had a wonderful week. We visited Meissen to see beautiful porcelain. We saw treasures that took our breath away. An evening at the re-built Semperoper for *La Bohème*. In contrast, after a long drive and crossing the Elbe by ferry, a production of *Der Freischütz* in the rain in a forest clearing. And the endless dreary blocks of flats from the days of Communism, now colour-washed and with window-boxes of geraniums.

Freia had been our *au pair* for eight months when Jonny was a baby. Now she and Manfred were grandparents. What a lovely friendship it has been.

Celebrations

One advantage of living in a village is the village hall. The Icklesham Memorial Hall was ideal for gatherings of the wider family for celebration parties.

At a Parents' Evening at Sutton High School, Judy's formmistress had told us of our eight-year-old's contribution to a discussion about deprivation among children. They had talked about the Third World, and then about their own situation. "Some children have no aunties and uncles. That means they have no cousins. So I think they're deprived." We would all agree with that!

And so we had some very happy gatherings, for our Ruby Wedding and for my 80th birthday.

We did celebrate our Golden Wedding, but inevitably we all had a huge feeling of loss. Our dear Jon had died in December 1999. He had made a brave fight against leukaemia. Life could never be the same for any of us, especially for his own family.

A celebration of a different kind was in 2001: a Jubilee Eucharist to celebrate the 50 years since my Ordination as Priest in Chichester Cathedral. We had a wonderful church-full, with friends from far-off Horsham and Beddington days joining the family and friends from nearer home. Bishop Peter did me the honour of travelling up from Somerset to preach. He and his twin brother Michael had been servers at St Mary's, Eastbourne, when I was curate there. We had some of my favourite hymns, including *Angel voices ever singing*, and Bishop Bell's hymn *Christ is the King*, and ended with some of the family joining the augmented choir for Stanford's *Te Deum*. And as we left the church a recording of a peal from the bells of St Mary's, Beddington, rang out joyfully across the valley. A memorable day.

Westminster Abbey

I continued as a Duty Clergyman at the Abbey. Frances used to come up with me. We occupied a flat in Little Cloister, courtesy of the Dean and Chapter. She would take advantage of being in town to go shopping and go to spend time with Judy and Simon in Alton. We usually finished the week with an excellent meal at the *Vitello D'Oro* having saved the week's Luncheon Vouchers. And then we would enjoy the weekend with my sister Elizabeth in Holly Village, Highgate. She would plan for church-going on Sundays: the Temple Church, the Chapel Royal and once, memorably, to hear Eric James preach at Gray's Inn.

At the Abbey there was a great variety of happenings. One year we were there for the Judges' service. The nave was cleared of chairs. There gathered hundreds of judges in full rig along with many other legal personages. They were thick on the ground, and I had to get past them to take a midweek Communion service in Henry VII chapel. No problem said Mr Powell, the Dean's verger. He took his silver verge in outstretched hand and just walked, with me and Frances behind him. The judges obligingly made a pathway for us like a crossing of the Red Sea. The judges then walked across from the Abbey to the House of Lords. Sniffer dogs much in evidence as the IRA was active at that time.

My duty weeks were usually in October. This meant that I was often there for St Edward the Confessor's Day, when all visitors were treated as pilgrims (i.e. no charges to visit the royal chapels) and many Communion services were held at the shrine.

We were fortunate to be there for some of the big services. Overseas visitors, annoyed to find the Abbey closed, could hardly believe their luck when they realised that they would see the Queen and the Duke of Edinburgh arrive at the Great West Door.

In 1992 there was the service to commemorate the 50th Anniversary of the Battle of El Alamein, with hundreds of veterans from the desert campaign. On this occasion the Queen was joined by the Prince and Princess of Wales. In the cloisters earlier in the day I had passed two men in deep conversation – Montgomery's son and Rommel's son, both to take part in the service.

1995 saw the restoration work on the Abbey's exterior completed. The scaffolding was down at last. It had taken 22 years, involving 1,500 craftsmen, craftswomen and workmen, and cost 25 million pounds. Another marvellous service. The Duke of Edinburgh, as President of the Westminster Abbey Trust, commended the work of the trust, and the Queen unveiled a new window to mark completion of the work.

The last big service we were up for was perhaps the most moving. This was the unveiling by the Queen of the Memorial to Innocent Victims. The stone lies outside the Great West Door, and was the inspiration of Dean Michael Mayne, soon to retire. Just as the Unknown Warrior's Grave honours the dead of the Great War, so this new memorial honours the millions of civilian victims of

Oppression, Violence and War. I missed the actual service, as I had been taking a Communion service in St Margaret's. But Frances stood outside the railings, with visitors from around the world, and watched as the Queen and Prince Philip laid a wreath of white flowers and rosemary at the memorial stone, with its simple lettering and the word "Remember" in the centre.

Later, as we were waiting in Dean's Yard to see the Queen leave, one of the vergers came up. He said I was needed in Jerusalem Chamber to meet Eric Lomax, the author of the PoW book *The Railway Man*. Lomax looked quite worn. It was Julian Harvey, wife of the Sub Dean Anthony Harvey, who had commanded the verger to find me. She had been at Downe House School during the war, when Aunt Dorothy was Head of Music, and remembered my name coming up in prayers for PoWs at Assembly.

Japanese Tourists

The Rev'd Uchida came to the Abbey once a week to greet Japanese tourists. He was friendly and knew of my experiences as a PoW. It was at the installation service of the new Dean that, in procession, I was actually walking with Uchida. Frances noticed this as rather a significant happening. In Japanese hands we had always to bow to guards. So when parties of Jap tourists appeared at the west door of the abbey I am afraid I rather delighted in stopping them in their tracks by doing a smart Jap-like stiff bow. They probably took it as "the done thing".

I had never joined any of the clubs and associations of FEPOWS (Far East PoWs). I had no inclination as a busy parish priest to use precious "days off" to relive those days. However, in 1992 an occasional worshipper at All Saints, Icklesham, asked if he would be seeing me at the Guildhall the following month. There was a Reception planned, and the Queen Mother would be present. Thanks to his good offices, I received an invitation, and Frances and I duly attended. This was the first public occasion to honour those who had suffered imprisonment in the Far East. The first group we spoke to had been in Changi, so I mentioned my friend,

Peter Ellis. This had an electrifying effect. They called friends over. "Come and meet the Padre. He knew our Mr Ellis." And so we heard of Peter constructing dental drills out of bicycle wheels and other bits and pieces. It was good to hear such positive memories, and we phoned Peter's widow that evening to tell her the story.

As a result of this day at Guildhall, where we enjoyed an excellent buffet lunch and heard Dame Vera Lynn sing some of the old favourites, I *did* join the London branch of the FEPOWS. And so I came to preach at St Martin's in the Fields for the annual service held on the Sunday nearest VJ Day. Things were rounded off, as it were, by this occasion, and lastly by receiving, with all other ex FEPOWS, the £10,000 *ex gratia* payment from the Government.

Poets' Corner

The first poet to be buried here was Geoffrey Chaucer in 1400. It is the scene of small gatherings, usually in the evening when visitors have gone, when a new name is added to the memorials. We were pleased to find that the 1989 stone commemorating John Clare, who died in 1864, was the work of John Skelton, who had sculpted the beautiful font in our Cathedral, and whom we had met at his home in Streat when we were visiting my brother George's grave.

There came a day when the Dean and Chapter at last got round to recognising Byron for memorialisation. After quite a touching service, an elderly, aristocratic lady came up to me – "at last DEAR LORD BYRON has been honoured!"

I had actually sung as a chorister in Poets' Corner when Thomas Hardy's ashes were interred. His heart was buried in Wessex, of course. But the story went around that a cat had got it first!

St Faith's Chapel

The dark door at the end of Poets' Corner leads into St Faith's Chapel. There, every morning when I was on duty, I would join Michael Mayne (Dean), Anthony Harvey (Sub Dean), and the

Canon in Residence, for meditation, mattins and communion. One's eye would fall on the lovely marble floor installed as a memorial to dear old Canon Perkins (1930), and then onwards to the mural of St Faith behind the altar (1250).

The chapel had been built into the very thick walls between the south transept and the chapter house. So one was within the very foundations of the Abbey, a place entirely congenial to me with my five years as a chorister (1926), and as duty clergyman from 1966 to 1996. It was that very door through which we went as choristers and through which I went 50 years later as priest.

In my accounts of captivity, release, repatriation and ordination I have admitted to the fact that nearly all my experiences and happenings, so far from being of my own engineering, seemed just to happen. My place was to respond. In all I was given a strong sense of the hand of God in my life. It is a source of amazement that His long purposes were being fulfilled. This of course included more than specifically "church" things, though these were of great privilege. But to have survived and then to meet Frances and raise our family! Well, as we sang at our wedding "Hast thou not seen how thy heart's wishes have been granted in what He ordaineth?"

Appendix 1
Timetable

Atom bomb 6th August 1945 to sailing date from Manila 10th October to Southampton 18th November 1945.

6th August	HIROSHIMA BOMB. 150 miles to south.	
3rd September	Jap surrender	
5th September	US Air force enter PoW camp	
7th September	Leave PoW camp.	Osaka to Yokohama 400 miles.
8th September	Yokohama hospital ship	Fujiyama (12,388 ft) 70 miles away.
14th September	Fly to Okinawa.	Yokohama to Okinawa 750 miles.
15th September	Fly to Manila	Okinawa to Manila 1,000 miles.
9th October	Leave Manila camp – start memoirs up ladder.	
10th October	San Francisco.	Manila to San Francisco 2,250 miles.
12th November	New York, Queen Mary.	San Francisco to New York 3,600 miles.
13th November	Sail for home.	
18th November	Southampton	New York to Southampton 3,700 miles.

Ticket No.1027HAHA issued in Manila camp. Manila to Southampton 16,000 miles.

Appendix 2
Glossary

A.P.C.	Associated Petroleum Co.
atap	roofing made of coconut fronds
benjo (Jap)	lavatory
Dammedaro	shout of disapproval (stronger than Kurrah!)
gippo	soup
godown	warehouse
gula malacca	sticky brown unrefined sugar
kempetai	much hated Jap military police
Kurrah!	shout of disapproval
tical	Siamese currency

Appendix 3

A Tribute by Imogen Clout at the Memorial Service held in St Mary's, Beddington

Imogen was an enthusiastic member of the Junior Church at St Mary's. She became a family law solicitor, but now works as a freelance writer and family mediator. She is mother of three teenagers and was licensed as a Reader in September 2006

The first time I met Mr Read, as he was to me then, was when I came here one Sunday morning for Junior Church. I remember being dressed in a peculiarly formal brown tweed suit – I was nine. I felt, probably because of the suit, uncomfortable and shy. And this tall person, with a lovely voice, made me welcome and wanted and I knew that I wanted to come again the next week. And I continued to come to this church until I grew up and left home.

Junior Church, in John's hands, was fun. And that was not necessarily the abiding characteristic of other Sunday Schools that I had been to. For a start we had a proper service – a cut-down version of Morning Prayer – so we were not patronised, and we did all sorts of things. We did a lot of plays. John taught us great chunks of bible stories by letting us act them. It was long, long afterwards that I learned of this as an "Ignatian" approach to the scripture – for us, it simply made the stories come alive. On fine days, we would go over the road and sit on the walls in the cemetery and act there. Curiously, the story that I have the clearest recollection of is Jezebel . . . This wasn't milk-and-water

113

religion. This wasn't soppy Sunday School, and it wasn't Sunday School where you had the moral of everything rammed down your throat.

And I think that this was John all over. I don't ever remember him being "preachy", or teaching at you. He simply was – he was the sweetest man I have ever met – not cloying or sickly sweet, but sweet like a good apple, sweet and full of flavour. His faith was manifest in everything that he was – the embodiment of a good man. And that bubbling sense of fun. Who else would think that a good way of commemorating Ascension Day would be to carve a piece of pear wood into a biscuit mould showing Jesus going up in a cloud, and commission the local baker to make enough biscuits for the whole of Beddington Infants School and the Junior Church to have one each? Ascension Day will always bring that to mind, for me. I think that he probably never forgot what it was like being a child. He knew what would appeal to small people, and treated us like people, too. And I saw this years later when I took my son to meet John and Frances, and Sam was immediately taken with the carvings and things that John had made in the garden that he showed him. Sam knew immediately, too, that this was a lovely man.

And he was such a good friend. When you're an awkward adolescent it's very precious to have a real friendship with an adult who doesn't patronise you or treat you in an avuncular fashion, but as another human soul. He encouraged me, he cherished me, he taught me. When I studied Greek he gave me the very precious gift of his big Liddell and Scott lexicon. It's a very treasured possession of mine. His example, his influence, led me into and confirmed me in my Christian faith, as I am sure he must have done with so many others. My debt of love to him is incalculable.

John is still very much alive to me, as perhaps you can tell. His laugh, his bright eyes, and his voice – I can still hear him singing Merbecke. All abiding memories. As Thomas More said: "Pray for me, as I will for thee, that we may meet merrily in heaven." I cannot think of anyone who is likely to be more merry when we meet again.

In one of the prayers for the departing soul there is a line "may the angels and saints come to meet you as you go forth from this life . . ." And when Frances told me of John's death, this line came to mind and I was sure that the angels had come running out to meet John, taken him by the hands and said "Come and play with us".